PRAŚNA U

With the Co
ŚANKARĀCĀRYA

Translated by
SWĀMĪ GAMBHĪRĀNANDA

Advaita Ashrama
(Publication Department)
5 Dehi Entally Road
Kolkata 700 014

Published by
Swami Mumukshananda
President, Advaita Ashrama
Mayavati, Champawat, Uttaranchal
from its Publication Department, Kolkata
Email: *mail@advaitaashrama.org*
Website: *www.advaitaashrama.org*

Fifth Impression, December 2005
3M3C

ISBN 81-7505-023-3

Printed in India at
Trio Process
Kolkata 700 014

PREFACE TO THE SECOND EDITION

This new edition of the *Praśna Upaniṣad* has been thoroughly revised by the author himself. In the matter of printing, to facilitate things for the reader, more space is given between the translation of the text and the translation of the *bhāṣya*. In the references, where only the figures without the name of any book occur, they refer to the *śloka* of this particular Upaniṣad.

PUBLISHER

PREFACE TO THE FIRST EDITION

The *Praśna Upaniṣad* is fourth in the series of Upaniṣads being published separately, taking each of them in its entirety from the earlier two-volume edition, *Eight Upaniṣads,* published by us. This has been preceded by the *Aitareya Upaniṣad,* the *Muṇḍaka Upaniṣad,* and the *Māṇḍūkya Upaniṣad* with the *Kārikā,* thus completing the publication of the four Upanisads in the second volume of *Eight Upaniṣads.*

In the translation of the commentary, the words quoted from the text by Śrī Śaṅkarācārya are given in italics. These are followed by commas and the English equivalents. Informative explanatory footnotes have been added wherever necessary.

This Upaniṣad derives its name from the six *praśnas* or questions it contains. It belongs to the AtharvaVeda, and very probably is of the Pippalāda *śākhā.* Śrī Śaṅkara refers to it as a Brāhmaṇa, complementary to the *Mantra Upaniṣad,* i.e. the *Muṇḍaka Upaniṣad,* which also belongs to the same Veda.

As the very name implies, the *Praśna Upaniṣad* discusses philosophical problems through the medium of questions and answers between six students and a sage, Pippalāda. The students approach him in accordance with the Vedic tradition, with sacrificial fuel in hand, in all humility, and with a desire to know the ultimate Truth. They are genuine seekers after Truth. They ask him various questions relating to the source of all beings, the number of deities, and the chief among them, the nature and function of Prāṇa, the vital force, the nature of waking, dream, and sleep states and the function of the senses in each of the states, meditation on the sacred syllable *Om*, and what it leads to, and finally the nature of the Supreme Persons, the conscious Being in man, Brahman, higher than whom there is nothing to be known. And to each of these questions, the sage gives a suitable answer, making it intelligible and easy of comprehension by means of interesting analogies and similes.

Like the *Taittirīya Upaniṣad,* it leads the aspirant gradually from the gross to the subtle principles of life and eventually points to the acme of spiritual perfection.

It is our hope that the *Praśna Upaniṣad* in this form will be welcomed by all lovers of our philosophical and spiritual lore.

Mayavati PUBLISHER

KEY TO TRANSLITERATION AND PRONUNCIATION

	Sounds like		Sounds like
अ	a o in s*o*n	ड	ḍ d
आ	ā a in m*a*ster	ढ	ḍh dh in go*dh*ood
इ	i i in *i*f	ण	ṇ n in u*n*der
ई	ī ee in f*ee*l	त	t French t
उ	u u in f*u*ll	थ	th th in *th*umb
ऊ	ū oo in b*oo*t	द	d th in *th*en
ऋ	ṛ somewhat between	ध	dh theh in brea*the h*ere
	r and ri	न	n n
ए	e a in ev*a*de	प	p p
ऐ	ai y in m*y*	फ	ph ph in loo*p-h*ole
ओ	o o in *o*ver	ब	b b
औ	au ow in n*ow*	भ	bh bḥ in a*bh*or
क	k k	म	m m
ख	kh ckh in blo*ckh*ead	य	y
ग	g g (hard)	र	r r
घ	gh gh in lo*g-h*ut	ल	l l
ङ	ṅ ng	व	v in a*v*ert
च	c ch (not k)	श	ś sh
छ	ch chh in cat*ch h*im	ष	ṣ sh in *sh*ow
ज	j j	स	s s
झ	jh dgeh in he*dgeh*og	ह	h h
ञ	ñ n (somewhat)		ṁ m in hu*m*
ट	ṭ t	:	ḥ half h in hu*h* !
ठ	ṭh th in an*t-h*ill		

LIST OF ABBREVIATIONS

A.G.	Ānanda Giri
Ai.	Aitareya Upaniṣad
Ai.Ā.	Aitareya Āraṇyaka
Ap.	Āpastaṁba Dharma-Sūtras
Bṛ.	Bṛhadāraṇyaka Upaniṣad
Ch.	Chāndogya Upaniṣad
G.	Bhagavad Gītā
Īś.	Īśā Upaniṣad
Jā.	Jābāla Upaniṣad
Ka.	Kaṭha Upaniṣad
Kau.	Kauṣītaki Upaniṣad
Ke.	Kena Upaniṣad
M.	Manu Saṁhitā
Mai.	Maitrāyaṇī Upaniṣad
Ma.Nā.	Mahānārāyaṇa Upaniṣad
Mā.	Māṇḍūkya Upaniṣad
Mbh.	Mahābhārata
Mu.	Muṇḍaka Upaniṣad
Muk.	Muktika Upaniṣad
Np.	Nārada-Parivrājaka Upaniṣad
Pr.	Praśna Upaniṣad
Ś.	Śaṅkarānanda
Śv.	Śvetāśvatara Upaniṣad
Tai.	Taittirīya Upaniṣad
Tai.Ā.	Taittirīya Āraṇyaka
Tai.B.	Taittirīya Brāhmaṇa
Tai.S.	Taittirīya Saṁhitā
Y.	Yajur-Veda

PRAŚNA UPANIṢAD

ॐ भद्रं कर्णेभिः श्रृणुयाम देवा
भद्रं पश्येमाक्षभिर्यजत्राः।
स्थिरैरङ्गैस्तुष्टुवाꣳसस्तनूभि-
र्व्यशेम देवहितं यदायुः॥
स्वस्ति न इन्द्रो वृद्धश्रवाः
स्वस्ति नः पूषा विश्ववेदाः।
स्वस्ति नस्तार्क्ष्यो अरिष्टनेमिः
स्वस्ति नो बृहस्पतिर्दधातु॥
ॐ शान्तिः शान्तिः शान्तिः॥

Om! O gods, may we hear auspicious words with the ears; while engaged in sacrifices, may we see auspicious things with the eyes; while praising (the gods) with steady limbs, may we enjoy a life that is beneficial to the gods.

May Indra of ancient fame be auspicious to us; may the supremely rich (or all-knowing) Pūṣā (god of the earth) be propitious to us; may Garuḍa, the destroyer of evil, be well-disposed towards us; may Bṛhaspati ensure our welfare.

Om! Peace! Peace! Peace!

PRAŚNA UPANIṢAD

FIRST QUESTION

This *brāhmaṇa*[1] is begun as an elaborate reiteration of the subject-matter already dealt with in the *mantra* portion.[2] The story in the form of questions and answers by the *ṛsis*, however, is meant for eulogising the knowledge. Knowledge is thus praised by showing that it can be acquired by those who are endowed with self-control and who undergo such disciplines as living in the teacher's house for a year under the vow of *brahmacarya*[3] and that it can be imparted by people who are almost omniscient like Pippalāda and others but not by a non-descript person. Moreover, *brahmacaryá* and other disciplines become obligatory from their reference (in the story):

ॐ सुकेशा च भारद्वाजः शैब्यश्च सत्यकामः सौर्यायणी

[1] i.e. this Upaniṣad occurring as the *brāhmana* or Vedic explanation of the *mantras* of the Muṇḍaka Upaniṣad.

[2] i.e. in the Muṇḍaka Upaniṣad which presented the knowledge of the Self and talked of two kinds of knowledge—the higher and the lower. The latter relates to both rites and meditation. Of these two kinds of lower knowledge, the first is dealt with in the *saṁhitā* portion of the Vedas, the second is elaborated in the Second and Third Questions of this Upaniṣad. The First Question clarifies the result of both rites and meditation so as to generate a dislike for them. The Fourth Question is meant as an elaboration of the two verses in the Muṇḍaka starting with 'As from a blazing fire' (Mu.II.i.1). The Fifth Question expands the meditation stated in the verse, '*Om* is the bow,' etc. (Mu.II.ii.4). The Sixth Question is for elucidating the remaining portion beginning with 'From this emerges Prāṇa' (Mu.II.i.3)—A.G.

[3] Celibacy and study of the Vedas with a pious attitude.

च गार्ग्यः कौसल्यश्चाश्वलायनो भार्गवो वैदर्भिः कबन्धी कात्यायनस्ते हैते ब्रह्मपरा ब्रह्मनिष्ठाः परं ब्रह्मान्वेषमाणा एष ह वै तत्सर्वं वक्ष्यतीति ते ह समित्पाणयो भगवन्तं पिप्पलादमुपसन्नाः ॥१॥

1. Sukeśā, son of Bharadvāja; Satyakāma, son of Śibi; the grandson of Sūrya, born of the family of Garga; Kausalya, son of Aśvala; a scion of the line of Bhṛgu, born in Vidarbha; and Kabandhī, descendant of Katya—all these, who were devoted to (the inferior) Brahman, engaged in realizing (the inferior) Brahman, and intent on a search of the supreme Brahman, approached with faggots in hand, the venerable Pippalāda with the belief, 'This one will certainly tell us all about It.'

Sukeśā by name, and (known as) *bhāradvājah*, (because he was) the son of Bharadvāja. *Śaibyaḥ*, the son of Śibi, who was Satyakāma by name. The son of Sūrya is Saurya, and Saurya's son is Sauryāyaṇī, the lengthening of *i* in Sauryāyaṇī being a Vedic licence; (and he was a) Gārgya, born in the line of Garga, Kausalya by name (and called) Āśvalāyana (because he was) the son of Aśvala. Bhārgava is one who was a scion of the line of Bhṛgu; and he was Vaidarbhi, being born in Vidarbha. Kabandhī by name; and he was Kātyāyana, a descendant (i.e. great-grandson) of Katya, and had his great-grandfather living, the suffix in the word being used to imply that sense. *Te ha ete*, these people who were such; were *brahmaparāh*, ever devoted to the inferior Brahman, mistaking that for the superior One; and they were *brahmaniṣṭhāḥ*, engaged in practices leading to Its attainment; and they were *param brahma anveṣamāṇāḥ*, intent on a search of the supreme Brahman. What is that (Brahman)? That which is eternal and a thing to be realized. They, who searched for that Brahman with the idea, 'For the sake of attaining It, we shall make efforts to our hearts content', approached a teacher for knowing about It, with the belief: '*Eṣaḥ ha vai tat sarvam vakṣyati*, this one will certainly tell us everything regarding It.' How did they go? *Samitpāṇayaḥ*, with loads of faggot in hand; *te ha*, those people; *upasannāḥ*, approached; *bhagavantam pippalādam*, the venerable Pippalāda, the teacher.

तान् ह स ऋषिरुवाच भूय एव तपसा ब्रह्मचर्येण श्रद्धया संवत्सरं संवत्स्यथ यथाकामं प्रश्नान् पृच्छत यदि विज्ञास्यामः सर्वं ह वो वक्ष्याम इति ॥२॥

2. To them the seer said, 'Live (here) for a year in a fitting manner, again with control over the senses and with *brahmacarya* and faith. Then put questions as you please. If we know, we shall explain all that you ask.'[1]

Tān, to them, who had approached (him) thus; *saḥ*, he; the *ṛṣiḥ*, seer; *uvāca ha*, said; —'Although you have already practised control of the senses, still *bhūyaḥ eva*, over again; you *saṁvatsyatha*, dwell here in a fitting manner; wholeheartedly serving your teacher, *saṁvatsaram*, for the period of a year; *tapasā*, with control of the senses; and especially *brahmacaryeṇa*, with *brahmacarya*; and *śraddhayā*, with faith, endowed with earnest belief in the truth (of the

[1] Ś. interprets *vaḥ* as 'to you'—'we shall explain everything to you.'

scriptures and the teacher's words). After that *pṛcchata praśnān*, put questions, with regard to anything that anyone (of you) may desire to know; *yathākāmam*, as you please, in accordance with the desire that each of you may entertain. *Yadi vijñāsyāmaḥ*, if we happen to know, what you ask; *vakṣyāmaḥ*, we shall explain; *sarvam ha vaḥ*, all, that you ask.' The word 'if' is used to express the absence of conceit, but not to betray ignorance or doubt, which fact is obvious from the solution of the questions (by him).

अथ कबन्धी कात्यायन उपेत्य पप्रच्छ। भगवन् कुतो ह वा इमाः प्रजाः प्रजायन्त इति ॥३॥

3. After that Kabandhī, descendant of Katya, having approached (him) asked, 'Venerable sir, from what indeed are all these beings born?'

Atha, after that, after the lapse of a year; *kabandhī-kātyāyanaḥ*, Kabandhī, great-grandson of Katya; *upetya*, having approached (him); *papraccha*, asked; '*Bhagavan*, O venerable sir; *kutaḥ ha vā*, from what indeed; *imāḥ prajāḥ*, these beings, counting from the Brāhmaṇas; *prajāyante*, are born?' The result obtained and the course merited by following the rites etc. in combination with the lower knowledge have to be stated; and hence this question.

तस्मै स होवाच प्रजाकामो वै प्रजापतिः स तपोऽतप्यत स तपस्तप्त्वा स मिथुनमुत्पादयते। रयिं च प्राणं चेत्येतौ मे बहुधा प्रजाः करिष्यत इति ॥४॥

4. To him he said: As is well known, the Lord of all creatures, having become desirous of progeny, He deliberated on (past Vedic) knowledge. Having brooded on that knowledge, He created a couple—food and Prāṇa—under the idea, 'These two will produce creatures for me in multifarious ways.'

Tasmai, to him, who had inquired thus; *saḥ ha uvāca*, he said; in order to solve that question: *Vai*, as is well known, having become *prajākāmaḥ*, desirous of creating progeny, for Himself—being filled with the idea, 'I shall create by becoming the soul of all'; *prajāpatiḥ*, the Lord of creatures—who had practised (meditation and rites conjointly in his earlier life) as already mentioned, and was full of that thought—evolved, at the commencement of a cycle (of creation), as Hiraṇyagarbha[1] by becoming the Lord of all moving and motionless creatures that were being created. (And having become Hiraṇyagarbha,) *saḥ tapaḥ atapyata*, He practised, deliberated on; the *tapas*, consisting in the knowledge which was acquired in the past life and which related to objects revealed by the Vedas. Then, *tapastaptvā*, after having practised *tapas* in that way, having revolved in His mind the Vedic knowledge; *saḥ*, He; *utpādayate*, created; *mithunam*, a couple that is instrumental to creation; (the couple, viz) *rayim ca*, the moon, the food; *prāṇam ca*, and Prāṇa, fire, the eater (the sun). After

[1] In His previous life He was a human aspirant meditating on Prajāpati (Hiraṇyagarbha) with the belief, 'I am Prajāpati, identified with all.' That intense meditation made Him Prajāpati at the beginning of the present cycle of creation. Even then the belief that He is Prajāpati persisted, and He had still in His mind all the Vedic knowledge acquired earlier.

creating the cosmic egg, He created the sun and the moon, under the idea, '*Etau*, these two, viz fire and moon, which are the eater and the eaten; *prajāḥ kariṣyataḥ*, will produce creatures; *bahudhā*, multifariously; *me*, for me.'[1]

आदित्यो ह वै प्राणो रयिरेव चन्द्रमा रयिर्वा एतत् सर्वं यन्मूर्तं चामूर्तं च तस्मान्मूर्तिरेव रयिः ॥५॥

5. The sun is verily Prāṇa, and food is verily the moon. Whatever is gross or subtle is but food. The gross, as distinguished from that (subtle), is certainly food (of the subtle).

Of these, *ādityaḥ ha vai*, the sun, verily; is *prāṇaḥ*, Prāṇa—the eater, fire; *rayiḥ eva*, the food is verily; *candramā*, the moon; *rayiḥ* is certainly the food and it is the moon. That which is the eater and that which is the food are but one; they are but Prajāpati who has become the couple, the distinction being made from the standpoint of superiority and inferiority. How? *Etat sarvam*, all this; *rayiḥ vai*, is but food. All of what? *Yat mūrtam*, whatever is formed, gross; *ca amūrtam*, and whatever is formless, subtle; all gross and subtle things, which constitute the food and the eater, are but *rayiḥ*, food. That *mūrtiḥ*, gross; which is different *tasmāt*, from that, from the subtle, which

[1] He projected the couple, the sun and the moon, and became identified with it. Then He created the year that is dependent on that couple, and became identified with the year. Thus successively He produced and became identified with the half-year, month, fortnight, day and night; rice, barley, and other foodstuff; semen and creatures. *Prāṇa* and *rayi* convey the ideas of energy and matter.

is wholly distinct; is indeed *rayiḥ*, food, since it is eaten up by the formless.[1]

Similarly, the formless Prāṇa (life), the eater, is also everything that is eaten, and hence it is all. How?

अथादित्य उदयन्यत्प्राचीं दिशं प्रविशति तेन प्राच्यान्
प्राणान् रश्मिषु संनिधत्ते। यद्दक्षिणां यत् प्रतीचीं यदुदीचीं
यदधो यदूर्ध्वं यदन्तरा दिशो यत् सर्वं प्रकाशयति तेन सर्वान्
प्राणान् रश्मिषु संनिधत्ते ॥६॥

6. Now then, the fact that the sun, while rising, enters into the eastern direction, thereby it absorbs into its rays all the creatures in the east. That it enters into the south, that it enters into the west, that it enters into the north, that it reaches the nadir and the zenith, that it enters the intermediate points of the zodiac, that it illumines all, thereby it absorbs all living things into its rays.

Atha, now then; *yat*, the fact that; *ādityaḥ udayan*, the sun, as it rises up, as it comes within the vision of creatures; *praviśati*, enters (that is to say,) pervades through its own light; *prācīm diśam*, the eastern quarter; *tena*, thereby, by that self-expansion—because these are pervaded by it; it *saṁnidhatte*, absorbs; *raśmiṣu*, into its rays which are but its own pervasive light; *prācyān prāṇān*, all that lives in, all creatures that happen to be included in, the eastern

[1] When no distinction of superior or inferior is made, then everything may be classed as food, for everything is absorbed by something else. But when the distinction is made, the gross gets absorbed in the subtle and is to be considered as food.

quarter, they being pervaded by its light; that is to say, it makes them one with itself. Similarly, *yat*, the fact that; it enters into the *dakṣiṇām*, southern direction; *yat pratīcīm*, that it enters into the western direction; *yat udīcīm*, that it enters into the northern direction; *yat*, that it enters into; *adhaḥ ūrdhvam*, the nadir, the zenith; *yat antarāḥ diśaḥ*, that it enters into the inter-spaces, the other points of the zodiac; *yat ca prakāśayati*, and the fact that it illumines; *sarvam*, all other things; *tena*, thereby, by that pervasion through its own light; it *saṃnidhatte*, absorbs; *raśmiṣu*, into the rays; *sarvān prāṇān*, all living things that exist in the different directions.

स एष वैश्वानरो विश्वरूपः प्राणोऽग्निरुदयते। तदेतदृचाऽभ्युक्तम् ॥७॥

7. That very one rises up who is Prāṇa and fire, who is identified with all creatures and who is possessed of all forms. This very one that has been referred to, is spoken of by the *mantra*:

Saḥ eṣaḥ, that very one, the eater; who is *prāṇaḥ vaiśvānaraḥ*, Prāṇa (life) identified with all creatures; and who is *viśvarūpaḥ*, possessed of all forms, being embodied in the universe; that is Prāṇa and *agniḥ*, fire. That eater, again, *udayate*, rises, every day, absorbing into himself all the cardinal points. *Etat tat*, this very entity that has been referred to above; is also *abhyuktam*, spoken of; *ṛcā*, by the (following) *mantra*:

विश्वरूपं हरिणं जातवेदसं
परायणं ज्योतिरेकं तपन्तम्।

सहस्ररश्मिः शतधा वर्तमानः
प्राणः प्रजानामुदयत्येष सूर्यः ॥८॥

8. (The realizers of Brahman knew) the one that is possessed of all forms, full of rays, endowed with illumination, the resort of all, the single light (of all), and the radiator of heat. It is the sun that rises—the sun that possesses a thousand rays, exists in a hundred forms and is the life of all creatures.

The enlightened realizers of Brahman knew, as their own soul, that sun that is *viśvarūpam*, possessed of all forms; *hariṇam*, full of rays; *jātavedasam*, endowed with enlightenment; *parāyaṇam*, the resort of all lives; *ekam jyotiḥ*, the only one light, which is the 'eye' of all beings; and *tapantam*, the radiator of heat. Who is that whom they knew? It is *eṣaḥ*, this; *sūryaḥ*, sun; that *udayati*, rises;—(the sun that is) *sahasraraśmiḥ*, possessed of a thousand rays; *śatadhā vartamānaḥ*, that exists in a hundred (i.e. many) ways, in conformity with the difference of the creatures; and that is *prāṇaḥ prajānām*, the life of creatures.

It is being explained how this single pair—constituted by that which is the moon, the gross, the food (on the one hand), and that which is the formless Prāṇa, the eater, the sun (on the other)—could produce the creatures:

संवत्सरो वै प्रजापतिस्तस्यायने दक्षिणं चोत्तरं च। तद्ये ह वै तदिष्टापूर्ते कृतमित्युपासते ते चान्द्रमसमेव लोकमभिजयन्ते। त एव पुनरावर्तन्ते तस्मादेत ऋषयः प्रजाकामा

दक्षिणं प्रतिपद्यन्ते । एष ह वै रयिर्यः पितृयाणः ॥९॥

9. The year is verily the Lord of creatures. Of Him there are two Courses, the Southern and the Northern. As to that, those who follow in that way the sacrifices and public good etc. that are products of action, conquer, verily, the world of the moon. It is they who come back. (Since this is so), hence these seers of heaven, who are desirous of progeny, attain the Southern Course. This which is the Course of the Manes is verily food.

That (couple) itself is the time called *saṁvatsaraḥ*, the year; (and that again is) *prajāpatiḥ*, the Lord of creatures; for the year is brought about by that (pair), the year being but a collection of the lunar days (*tithi*) and solar days and nights, caused by the moon and the sun. Being non-different from the food and Prāṇa, the year is said to be verily identical with that couple. How is that so? *Tasya*; of that Lord of the creatures, who the year is; there are *ayane*, two Courses; *dakṣiṇam ca uttaram ca*, the Southern and the Northern. These, indeed, are the two well-known Courses consisting each of six months, along which the sun moves to the south and the north, ordaining the results for those who perform rites alone as well as for those who undertake rites along with meditation. How is that? *Tat*, as to that; *ye ha vai*, those who, from among people counting from the Brāhmaṇas; *upāsate*, follow; *tat*, in that way; *iṣṭāpūrte*, sacrifices and public good; *iti*, etc.; that are *kṛtam*, products of action, but who do not follow the uncreated Eternal—the second *tat*, meaning 'in that way,' being used adverbially—; (they) *abhijayante*, conquer; *cāndramasam lokam*, world of the moon, the world constituted by food which is a portion, called *rayi* (food), of the Lord of the creatures who comprises a pair. This is so because the moon is *kṛta*, a result of action. When the result of action is exhausted there, *te eva punaḥ āvartante*, it is they who come back again; for it has been said, 'They enter into this or an inferior world' (Mu.I.ii.10). Since in this way *ete*, these; *ṛṣayaḥ*, seers of heaven; *prajākāmāḥ*, who are desirous of progeny, the householders; attain (the world of) the moon—the Lord of creatures who is identified with food—as the result of their sacrificial and pious acts; *tasmāt*, therefore; they *pratipadyante*, attain; *dakṣiṇam*, the Southern Course, that is to say, the moon, suggested by the (term) Southern Course, which is earned by themselves. *Eṣaḥ ha vai rayiḥ*, this indeed is food; *yaḥ pitṛyāṇaḥ*, which is the path of the Manes, that is to say, the (world of the) moon, as suggested by the (term) Path of the Manes.

अथोत्तरेण तपसा ब्रह्मचर्येण श्रद्धया विद्ययाऽऽत्मानमन्विष्या-
दित्यमभिजयन्ते। एतद्वै प्राणानामायतनमेतदमृतमभयमेतत्
परायणमेतस्मान्न पुनरावर्तन्त इत्येष निरोधस्तदेष श्लोकः ॥१०॥

10. Again, by searching for the Self through the control of the senses, *brahmacarya*, faith and meditation, they conquer the sun (by proceeding) along the Northern Course. This is the resort of all that lives; this is indestructible; this is fearless; this is the highest goal, for from this they do not come back. This is unrealizable (to the ignorant). Pertaining to this here is a verse:

Atha, again; *uttareṇa*, by proceeding along the Northern Course; they *abhijayante*, conquer; that part of the Lord of creatures which is Prāṇa, the eater, the sun. Through what? *Anviṣya*, by searching for, i.e. knowing; *ātmānam*, the Self, that is Prāṇa, the sun, the Self of the moving and unmoving; as 'I am this (Prāṇa that is the sun)'; *tapasā*, through the control of the senses; and especially *brahmacaryeṇa*, through *brahmacarya*; *śraddhayā*, through faith; and *vidyayā*, through meditation, with the idea of the identity of oneself with the Lord of creatures; they *abhijayante*, conquer, attain; *ādityam*, the sun. *Etat vai*, this indeed; is the common *āyatanam*, resort; *prāṇānām*, of all that lives.[1] *Etat*, this one; is *amṛtam*, indestructible; and because of that fact, this is *abhayam*, free from fear, not subject to the fear of waxing and waning like the moon. *Etat parāyaṇam*, this one is the supreme goal, for the meditators as well as for the men who combine meditation with rites; *iti*, for; *etasmāt na punaḥ āvartante*, from this (they) do not return, like the others who perform rites alone. *Eṣaḥ*, this one; is *nirodaḥ*, unrealizable, to the ignorant; for the ignorant are shut off from the sun. These people do not attain the year, the sun, the Self, which is Prāṇa. For that year, identical with time, proves an obstruction to the ignorant. *Tat*, pertaining to this idea; *eṣaḥ ślokaḥ*, here is a verse:

पञ्चपादं पितरं द्वादशाकृतिं
दिव आहुः परे अर्धे पुरीषिणम् ।
अथेमे अन्य उ परे विचक्षणं
सप्तचक्रे षडर आहुरर्पितमिति ॥११॥

11. Some talk of (this sun) as possessed of five feet, as

[1] Or 'all the organs—eyes etc.', according to Ś.

the father, as constituted by twelve limbs, and as full of water in the high place above the sky. But there are these others who call him the omniscient and say that on him, as possessed of seven wheels and six spokes, is fixed (the whole universe).

The calculators of time *āhuḥ*, call him; *pañcapādam*, possessed of five feet, the five seasons being the feet, as it were, of the sun as identified with the year; for he revolves with the help of those seasons, which are as though his feet. In this imagery, late autumn and winter are taken as but one season. (They call him) *pitaram*, father. He is the father because he is the generator of all. (They call him) *dvādaśākṛtim*, as possessed of twelve forms —he who has the twelve months as his limbs, or he who is made an embodied being by the twelve months. They call him *purīṣiṇam*, full of water;[1] *ardhe pare dive*, in the place above heaven (i.e. sky)[2], that is to say, in the third place which is above the sky. *U*, but; on the other hand *anye ime pare*, these others, other calculators of time; (*āhuḥ*, call) that very one, *vicakṣaṇam*, adept, omniscient. (And they) *āhuḥ*, say; that like spokes fixed on the nave of a wheel the whole universe is *arpitam*, fixed; on him who, as the embodiment of time, is ever on the move;—on him *saptacakre*, who is possessed of seven wheels, in the form of seven horses; and *ṣaḍare*, who is endowed with six spokes, the six seasons. Whether he be possessed of five feet and twelve limbs or seven wheels and six spokes, from either point of view it is the year, the

[1] The sun causes clouds, from which rain comes.

[2] It is third counting from this earth, the second being the sky. Heaven in this context does not mean the dwelling place of the gods, but the sky; else, there will be a conflict with the commentary—'in the *third* place which is above the sky.'—A.G.

embodiment of time, the Lord of all creatures, constituted even by the sun and the moon, which is the cause of the world.

He by whom the whole world is sustained is called the year, the Lord of all creatures; and He is wholly evolved into the twelve months which are His limbs:

मासो वै प्रजापतिस्तस्य कृष्णपक्ष एव रयिः शुक्लः प्राण-
स्तस्मादेत ऋषयः शुक्ल इष्टं कुर्वन्तीतर इतरस्मिन् ॥१२॥

12. The month verily is the Lord of all creatures. The dark fortnight is His food, and the bright His Prāṇa. Therefore these seers perform the sacrifices in the bright fortnight. The others perform it in the other.

Māsaḥ vai, the month verily; which is also *prajāpatiḥ*, the Lord of all creatures, as described before; is constituted by a pair. *Tasya*, of him, of that Lord of creatures who is marked by the month; one part, viz *kṛṣṇapakṣaḥ*, the dark fortnight; is *rayiḥ*, food, the moon; the other part, viz *śuklaḥ*, the bright (fortnight); is Prāṇa, the sun, the eater, fire. Since they look upon Prāṇa, identified with the bright fortnight, as everything, therefore, *ete ṛṣayaḥ*, these seers, who realize Prāṇa; *śukle iṣṭam kurvanti*, perform their sacrifice (really) in the bright fortnight, even though they may be performing it in the dark half, because they do not perceive any dark fortnight existing apart from Prāṇa. On the other hand, whereas the others do not see Prāṇa, and as a result see only that which is marked by darkness and obstructs vision. Therefore *itare*, the others;

kurvanti, perform; (their sacrifice, really) *itarasmin*, in the other half, in the dark fortnight, although they may be doing so in the bright half.

अहोरात्रो वै प्रजापतिस्तस्याहरेव प्राणो रात्रिरेव रयिः प्राणं वा एते प्रस्कन्दन्ति ये दिवा रत्या संयुज्यन्ते ब्रह्मचर्यमेव तद्यद्रात्रौ रत्या संयुज्यन्ते ॥१३॥

13. Day and night are verily the Lord of all creatures. Day is surely His prāṇa and night is certainly the food. Those who indulge in passion during the day, waste away Prāṇa. That they give play to passion at night is as good as celibacy.

The Lord of all creatures, marked by the month, gets again circumscribed by the day and night which are His own limbs. *Ahorātraḥ vai prajāpatiḥ*, day and night are verily the Lord of all creatures, just as before. *Tasya*, of Him, too; *ahar eva prāṇaḥ*, the day is surely Prāṇa, the eater and fire; *rātriḥ eva rayiḥ*, night is certainly the food, just as before. *Ete*, these people; *praskandanti*, eject, exhaust, waste away by separating from themselves; *prāṇam*, Prāṇa, identified with day. Who are they? *Ye*, those who, the fools who; *divā*, during the day time; *samyujyante ratyā*, indulge in passion, that is to say unite with women who cause passion. . . . Since this is so, therefore that should not be done. This is a prohibition enjoined by the way. The fact that they *samyujyante ratyā*, give play to passion; *rātrau*, at night, at (the proper) time; *tat*, that; is *brahmacaryam eva*, as good as continence. Since this has been praised, therefore, this too is an injunction enunciated in passing, that it is one's duty to unite with one's wife in due time. As for the relevant topic, it is this: That Lord of all creatures, who has evolved into day and night, exists as identified with such food as rice and barley.

अन्नं वै प्रजापतिस्ततो ह वै तद्रेतस्तस्मादिमाः प्रजाः प्रजायन्त इति ॥१४॥

14. Food is nothing but the Lord of all creatures. From that indeed issues that human seed. From that are born these beings.

Evolving thus in succession, *prajāpatiḥ*, the Lord of all creatures; became that *annam vai*, food to be sure. How? *Tataḥ ha vai*, from that (food) indeed, is formed; *tat retas*, that human seed, which is the origin of creatures. *Tasmāt*, from that (seed), when deposited in a woman; *prajāyante*, are born; *imāḥ prajāḥ*, these creatures, distinguished as men and others. The question that was raised, 'From what indeed are the beings born?', has thus been answered by saying that these creatures are born by passing in succession through the pairs starting with the sun and the moon and ending with day and night, and then by proceeding through food, blood and semen.

तद्ये ह वै तत् प्रजापतिव्रतं चरन्ति ते मिथुनमुत्पादयन्ते। तेषामेवैष ब्रह्मलोको येषां तपो ब्रह्मचर्यं येषु सत्यं प्रतिष्ठितम् ॥१५॥

15. This being so, those who undertake the well-known

vow of the Lord of all creatures, beget both sons and daughters. For them alone is this world of the moon in whom there are that vow and continence, and in whom is found for ever avoidance of falsehood.

Tat, this being so; *ye*, those, the householders who—*ha* and *vai* are two indeclinables calling up to mind some well-known fact—; *caranti*, undertake; *tat prajāpativratam*, that vow of the Lord of all creatures, consisting in uniting with one's wife at the proper time, for them this is the visible result. What is that? *Te*, they; *utpādayante*, beget; *mithunam*, a pair, both son and daughter. This unseen result consisting in *eṣaḥ brahmalokaḥ*, this world of Brahman, the world of the moon, that is indicated by the Path of the Manes; is *teṣām eva*, for those people alone, for those who undertake sacrifices and public good and offer gifts; *yeṣām*, in whom; there are *tapas*, vows as for instance those vows undertaken by one who has completed his study; *brahmacaryam*, continence, consisting in not living with one's wife at times other than the proper season; *yeṣu*, in whom, again; *satyam*, truthfulness, avoidance of falsehood, *pratiṣṭhitam*, exists invariably for ever.

तेषामसौ विरजो ब्रह्मलोको न येषु जिह्ममनृतं न माया चेति ॥१६॥

इति प्रश्नोपनिषदि प्रथमः प्रश्नः ॥

16. For them is that taintless world of Brahman, in whom there is no crookedness, no falsehood, and no dissimulation.

As for the Northern Course, marked out by the sun, which consists of self-identification with Prāṇa; and is *virajaḥ*, pure, not tainted like the lunar Brahmaloka and not subject to waxing and waning; *asau*, that one; is *teṣām*, for them. For whom? That is being said: (For those) *na yeṣu jihmam*, in whom there is no fraud, no crookedness, unlike the householders in whom it becomes inevitable owing to the exigencies of many contradictory social situations. Also, those in whom *anṛtam*, falsehood, does not become unavoidable as it is with of householders in the course of play or merriment. Similarly, those in whom, unlike the householders, there does not exist any *māyā*. *Māyā*, dissimulation, is a kind of false behaviour consisting in showing oneself publicly in some way and acting quite contrariwise. For those competent persons—the *brahmacāris* (celibates), forest-dwellers, and mendicants—in whom such blemishes as *māyā* do not exist because there is no occasion for them; is this untainted world of Brahman, just in consonance with the disciplines they undertake. This is the goal for those who undertake rites in conjunction with meditation. But the Brahmaloka indicated by the moon, mentioned earlier, is for those who perform rites alone.

SECOND QUESTION

It has been said that Prāṇa is the eater and the Lord of all creatures. It has to be determined how He is the Lord of all creatures as well as the eater in this body. Hence is the Question begun.[1]

अथ हैनं भार्गवो वैदर्भिः पप्रच्छ। भगवन् कत्येव देवाः प्रजां विधारयन्ते कतर एतत् प्रकाशयन्ते कः पुनरेषां वरिष्ठ इति ॥१॥

1. Next a scion of the line of Bhṛgu, born in Vidarbha, asked him, 'Adorable sir, how many in fact are the deities that sustain a creature? Which among them exhibit this glory? Which, again, is the chief among them?'

Atha ha, next in order; *bhārgavaḥ vaidarbhiḥ*, a scion of the line of Bhṛgu, who was born in Vidarbha; *papraccha*, asked; *enam*, this one: *Bhagavan*, O adorable sir; *kati eva devāḥ*, how many deities indeed; *vidhārayante*, chiefly sustain; *prajām*, a creature, so far as the body is concerned. *Katare*, which of them, which of those deities divided among the organs of sense and action; *prakāśayante*, exhibit; *etat*, this, this manifestation of their own glory; *kaḥ punaḥ*, which, again; is *variṣṭhaḥ*, the chief; *eṣām*, among these that exist as body and organs.

तस्मै स होवाचाकाशो ह वा एष देवो वायुरग्निरापः

[1] In this chapter it will be shown that Prāṇa is the chief, the eater, and the Lord of all creation. The next chapter will enjoin His meditation.

पृथिवी वाङ्मनश्चक्षुः श्रोत्रं च। ते प्रकाश्याभिवदन्ति वयमेतद्-
बाणमवष्टभ्य विधारयामः ॥२॥

2. To him he said: Space in fact is this deity, as also are air, fire, water, earth, the organ of speech, mind, eye, and ear. Exhibiting their glory they say, 'Unquestionably it is we who hold together this body by not allowing it to disintegrate.'

Tasmai, to him, who had asked thus; *saḥ*, he; *uvāca ha*, said: *Ākāśaḥ ha vai eṣaḥ devaḥ*, space is in fact this deity; as also are *vāyuḥ*, air; *agniḥ*, fire; *āpaḥ*, water; *pṛthivī*, earth—these five elements that are the material causes of the body; (and) *vāk*, speech; *manas*, mind; *cakṣuḥ*, eye; *śrotram*, ear. These and others that are the organs of action and knowledge, *te*, they (that is to say), the gods (presiding over these and) identifying themselves with the body and organs; *abhivadanti prakāśya*, speak by way of exhibiting their own glory, while vying for pre-eminence. How do they speak? 'It is *vayam*, we; who, like the pillars of a palace, *vidhārayāmaḥ*, unquestionably hold together; *etat bāṇam*, this aggregate of body and organs; *avaṣṭabhya*, by holding it aloft, and not allowing it to be disintegrated.' The idea of each one is this: 'It is indeed by me alone that this aggregate is upheld.' This is the idea.

तान् वरिष्ठः प्राण उवाच। मा मोहमापद्यथाऽहमेवैतत्
पञ्चधाऽऽत्मानं प्रविभज्यैतद्बाणमवष्टभ्य विधारयामीति तेऽश्रद्द-
धाना बभूवुः ॥३॥

3. To them the chief Prāṇa said, 'Do not be deluded. It is I who do not allow it to disintegrate by sustaining it by dividing myself fivefold.' They remained incredulous.

Tān, to them, to those who had such egotism; *variṣṭhaḥ prāṇaḥ*, the chief Prāṇa; *uvāca*, said: '*Mā āpadyatha moham*, do not fall into delusion, do not cherish in this way any vanity resulting from non-discrimination; for *aham eva*, it is I who; *vidhārayāmi etat bāṇam avaṣṭabhya*, sustain this aggregate of body and organs by not allowing it to disintegrate; I support it, *pañcadhā ātmānam pravibhajya*, by dividing myself fivefold, by dividing my functions into those of the outgoing breath etc.' Although he said so, still *te*, they; *babhūvuḥ*, remained; *aśraddadhānāḥ*, incredulous, thinking, 'How can this be so?'

सोऽभिमानादूर्ध्वमुत्क्रमत इव तस्मिन्नुत्क्रामत्यथेतरे सर्व एवोत्क्रामन्ते तस्मिꣳश्च प्रतिष्ठमाने सर्व एव प्रातिष्ठन्ते। तद्यथा मक्षिका मधुकरराजानमुत्क्रामन्तं सर्वा एवोत्क्रामन्ते तस्मिꣳश्च प्रतिष्ठमाने सर्वा एव प्रातिष्ठन्त एवं वाङ्मनश्चक्षुः श्रोत्रं च ते प्रीताः प्राणं स्तुन्वन्ति ॥४॥

4. He appeared to be rising up (from the body) out of indignation. As he ascended, all the others without exception ascended immediately; and when he remained quiet, all others too remained in position. Just as in the world, all the bees take to flight in accordance as the king of the bees takes to his wings, and they settle down as he does so, similarly, did speech, mind, eye, ear, etc. behave. Becoming delighted, they (began to) praise Prāṇa.

Noticing their incredulity, *saḥ*, that Prāṇa; on his part, became indifferent, and *utkramate iva*, seemed to rise up, seemed to have risen up from this (body); *abhimānāt*, out of indignation. What followed his ascent is being made vivid with the help of an illustration. *Tasmin utkrāmati*, when he began to rise up; *atha*, then, immediately after; *itare sarve eva*, all the others without exception, all the organs such as the eye; *utkrāmante*, ascend(ed); *ca tasmin pratiṣṭhamāne*, and when he, the Prāṇa, stayed on, remained quiet, did not rise up; *sarve eva prātiṣṭhante*, all of them remain(ed) quietly in position. *Tat*, with regard to this matter, the illustration is: *Yathā*, as; *loke*, in the world; *makṣikāḥ*, bees; *sarvāḥ eva*, all of them; *utkrāmante*, take to flight; *madhukararājānam utkrāmantam*, as the king of bees, their own king, takes to his wings; *ca sarvāḥ eva prātiṣṭhante*, and all settle down; *tasmin pratiṣṭhamāne*, as he settles down—. As is this illustration, so (did) *vāk*, speech; *manaḥ*, mind; *cakṣuḥ*, eye; *śrotram*, ear; and others (behave). *Te*, they; having given up their lack of faith, and having realized the greatness of Prāṇa, and becoming *prītāḥ*, delighted; *stunvanti prāṇam*, praise Prāṇa.

How did they praise?

एषोऽग्निस्तपत्येष सूर्य
एष पर्जन्यो मघवानेष वायुः ।
एष पृथिवी रयिर्देवः
सदसच्चामृतं च यत् ॥५॥

5. This one (i.e. Prāṇa) burns as fire, this one is the sun, this one is the cloud, this one is Indra and air, this one is

the earth and food. This god is the gross and the subtle, as well as that which is nectar.

Eṣaḥ, this one, this Prāṇa; in the form of *agniḥ*, fire; *tapati*, burns. Similarly, he shines as *sūryaḥ*, the sun. So also, as *parjanyaḥ*, cloud; he *varṣati*, rains. Moreover, as *maghavān*, Indra, he protects the creatures and endeavours to kill the demons and ogres. *Esah*, this one; is *vāyuḥ*, air, diversified as different currents like *āvaha*, *pravaha*. Furthermore, *esah devaḥ*, this deity; is *pṛthivī*, the earth; (and) *rayiḥ*, food, of the whole world;[1] *sat*, the gross; *asat*, the subtle; *ca*, and; *yat amṛtam*, that which is nectar that ensures the sustenance of the gods. The point needs no further elaboration.

अरा इव रथनाभौ प्राणे सर्वं प्रतिष्ठितम् ।
ऋचो यजूꣳषि सामानि यज्ञः क्षत्रं ब्रह्म च ॥६॥

6. Like spokes on the hub of a chariot wheel, are fixed on Prāṇa all things—*ṛks*, *yajus*, *sāmas*, sacrifice, Kṣatriya and Brāhmaṇa.

Arāḥ iva rathanābhau, as spokes are fixed on the hub of a chariot wheel; so *sarvam*, everything, starting from faith and ending with name (VI.4); *pratiṣṭhitam*, is fixed; verily, *prāṇe*, on Prāṇa; during the time of the existence of the world. Similarly, the three kinds of *mantras*—*ṛcaḥ*, *ṛks*; *yajūṁṣi*, *yajus*; *sāmāni*, *sāmas*—(metrical, prose, and musical Vedic texts); and the *yajñaḥ*, sacrifice that is

[1] As the earth, He supports all; and as food, He nourishes all.

performed with those *mantras*; and the *kṣatram*, Kṣatriya caste that protects all; *ca*, and; even *brahma*, the Brāhmaṇa caste that is qualified for the performance of duties like sacrifice. This Prāṇa is everything.

प्रजापतिश्चरसि गर्भे त्वमेव प्रतिजायसे ।
तुभ्यं प्राण प्रजास्त्विमा बलिं हरन्ति
यः प्राणैः प्रतितिष्ठसि ॥७॥

7. It is verily you who move about in the womb as the Lord of creation, and it is you who take birth after the image of the parents. O Prāna, it is for you, who reside with the organs, that all these creatures carry presents.

Moreover, even He who is called *prajāpatiḥ*, the Lord of creatures; *tvam*, *eva*, is but you. It is you who *carasi*, move; *garbhe*, in the womb—of the father (as seed) and of the mother (as child); and (it is you, again, who) *pratijāyase*, take birth after the image of (the parents). Since you are the Lord of creatures, your parenthood is a pre-established fact. The purport is this: You, Prāna, who are one, are identical with all in the guise of the form of all bodies and embodied beings. *Prāṇa*, O Prāṇa; it is *tubhyam*, to you alone; that *imāh prajāh*, all these creatures that there are, counting from human beings; *balim haranti*, carry presents, through the eyes etc. Since it is you *yah*, who; *pratitisthasi*, reside; *prāṇaih*, with the organs, eyes etc., in all the bodies, therefore it is proper that they should carry presents to you. As you are in fact the eater, so all else is food for you only.

देवानामसि वह्नितमः पितॄणां प्रथमा स्वधा ।
ऋषीणां चरितं सत्यमथर्वाङ्गिरसामसि ॥८॥

8. You are the best transmitter (of libation) to the celestials. You are the food-offering to the manes that precedes other offerings. You are the right conduct of the organs that constitute the essence of the body and which are known as the *atharvas*.

Moreover, you *asi*, are; *vahnitamaḥ*, the best carrier, the best transmitter, of libations; *devānām*, to the celestials, beginning with Indra. The *svadhā*, food-offering; made *pitṛṇām*, to the manes, in the obsequial rite called Nāndī-mukha in honour of the manes; that is the *prathamā*, first, that takes precedence over the other offerings in which the deities dominate[1]—of that food-offering also, it is you alone who carry it to the manes. This is the idea. Furthermore, it is you who *asi*, are; the *satyam caritam*, true, right, conduct, consisting in maintaining the body etc.; *ṛṣīṇām*, of the organs, such as the eyes etc.; *atharva- aṅgirasām*, which constitute the essence of the body, and which are called the *atharvas* according to the Vedic text, 'Prāṇa is indeed *atharvā*.'[2]

इन्द्रस्त्वं प्राण तेजसा रुद्रोऽसि परिरक्षिता ।
त्वमन्तरिक्षे चरसि सूर्यस्त्वं ज्योतिषां पतिः ॥९॥

9. O Prāṇa, you are Indra. Through your valour you are Rudra; and you are the preserver on all sides. You

[1] The reading is *deva-pradhāna* or *deva-pradāna*. The first reading is adopted in the translation. The second reading would give the meaning, 'Over the offering to the gods'. The Nāndī-mukha has to be performed before making the sacrifices to gods.

[2] Though Prāṇa is *atharvā* according to this quotation yet the sense-organs, which are but manifestations of Prāṇa, are also *atharvā*.

move in the sky—you are the sun, the Lord of all luminaries.

Further, *prāṇa*, O Prāṇa; *tvam*, you; are *indraḥ*, Indra, the supreme Lord. *Tejasā*, by valour; *asi*, you are; *rudraḥ*, Rudra, engaged in destroying the world. Again, during the time of the existence of the universe, you, in your benign aspect, are the *parirakṣitā*, preserver (of the universe) on every side. *Tvam*, you; *carasi*, move, for ever; *antarikṣe*, in the sky, by rising and setting. *Tvam*, you; are the *sūryaḥ*, sun; the *patiḥ*, lord; *joytiṣām*, of all the luminaries.

यदा त्वमभिवर्षस्यथेमाः प्राणते प्रजाः ।
आनन्दरूपास्तिष्ठन्ति कामायान्नं भविष्यतीति ॥१०॥

10. O Prāṇa, when you pour down (as rain), then these creatures of yours continue to be in a happy mood under the belief, 'Food will be produced to our hearts' content.'

Yadā, when; *tvam*, you; *abhivarṣasi*, pour down by becoming a rain cloud; *atha*, then; getting food, *imāḥ prajāḥ*, these creatures; *prāṇate*, live, that is to say, resort to activities characteristic of vitality. Or (reading *prāṇa te*, in place of *prāṇate*), *prāṇa*, O Prāṇa; at the very sight of the rain you pour down, *imāḥ prajāḥ te*, these creatures of yours—which are one with you and which are nourished by your food; *tiṣṭhanti*, continue to be; *ānandarūpāḥ*, like people possessed of happiness; their idea being this: '*Annam bhaviṣyati*, food will be produced; *kāmāya*, to our hearts' content.'

व्रात्यस्त्वं प्राणैकर्षिरत्ता विश्वस्य सत्पतिः।
वयमाद्यस्य दातारः पिता त्वं मातरिश्व नः ॥११॥

11. O Prāṇa, you are unpurified, you are the fire Ekarṣi, (you are) the eater, and you are the lord of all that exists. We are the givers of (your) food. O Mātariśvā, you are our father.

Besides, *prāṇa*, O Prāṇa; *tvam*, you; are *vrātyaḥ*, unpurified—having been born first, you had none to baptise you; the idea is that you are naturally pure. As the fire called *ekarṣiḥ*, Ekarṣi, that is well known among the followers of the Atharva-veda; you become the *attā*, eater, of all oblations. You are the *satpatiḥ viśvasya*, the lord of all that exists—*satpatiḥ*, being derived in the sense of the lord (*pati*) of what exists (*sat*). Or *satpatiḥ* may mean holy lord. *Vayam*, we, again; are *dātāraḥ*, the givers, to you; *ādyasya*, of food, of oblations that you partake of. *Mātariśva*, O Mātariśvā (Air); *tvam*, you; are *naḥ pitā*, our father (the word *mātariśva* being taken as a Vedic use for *mātariśvan*). Or, if the reading be *mātariśvanaḥ*, the meaning (of the sentence) will be: *Tvam*, you; are the *pitā*, father; *mātariśvanaḥ*, of Mātariśvā (Air)[1]. Hence also is established your fatherhood of the whole Universe.

या ते तनूर्वाचि प्रतिष्ठिता या श्रोत्रे या च चक्षुषि।
या च मनसि सन्तता शिवां तां कुरु मोत्क्रमीः ॥१२॥

[1] Since you are identified with *ākāśa* (space), the source of air.

12. Make calm that aspect of yours that is lodged in speech, that which is in the ear, that which is in the eye, and that which permeates the mind. Do not rise up.

To be brief, *yā tanūḥ te*, that aspect of yours; which is *pratiṣṭhitā*, lodged; *vāci*, in speech, which makes the effort of speaking as a speaker; *yā śrotre*, that which is in the ear; *ca yā cakṣuṣi*, and that which is in the eye; *ca yā*, and that which, the aspect which; is *santatā*, pervasive; *manasi*, in the mind, as acts of thinking etc.; *kuru*, make; *tām*, that (aspect); *śivām*, calm. *Mā utkramīḥ*, do not ascend, that is to say, do not make it inactive[1] by ascending.

प्राणस्येदं वशे सर्वं त्रिदिवे यत् प्रतिष्ठितम् ।
मातेव पुत्रान् रक्षस्व श्रीश्च प्रज्ञां च विधेहि न इति ॥१३॥

इति प्रश्नोपनिषदि द्वितीयः प्रश्नः ॥

13. All this (in this world), as also all that in heaven is under the control of Prāna. Protect us just as a mother does her sons, and ordain for us splendour and intelligence.

In short, whatever enjoyable thing there is in this world, *sarvam idam*, all this; is verily *prāṇasya vaśe*, under the control of Prāṇa. And Prāṇa is even the ruler and protector of *yat*, whatever—in the form of enjoyment for gods and others; is *pratiṣṭhitam*, located; *tridive*, in the third heaven, in the form of enjoyment for gods and others. Hence, *rakṣasva*, protect us; *mātā iva putrān*, as a mother does her sons. Since all the glories natural to the Brāhmaṇas and

[1] This is according to A.G. Some translate it as *unholy*.

Kṣatriyas are at your disposal, therefore *vidhehi naḥ*, ordain for us; *śrīḥ ca* (is the same as *śriyaḥ ca*), all splendour; *prajñām ca*, and intelligence, that accrue from your continuance. This is the meaning. Thus, inasmuch as the greatness of Prāṇa has been disclosed by the organs such as speech through His praise as the all-pervasive entity, therefore, Prāṇa is ascertained as the Lord of creatures and the eater.

THIRD QUESTION

अथ हैनं कौसल्यश्चाश्वलायनः पप्रच्छ। भगवन् कुत एष प्राणो जायते कथमायात्यस्मिञ्शरीर आत्मानं वा प्रविभज्य कथं प्रातिष्ठते केनोत्क्रमते कथं बाह्यमभिधत्ते कथमध्यात्म-मिति ॥१॥

1. Then Kausalya, son of Aśvala, asked him, 'O venerable sir, from where is this Prāṇa born? How does he come into this body? How again does he dwell by dividing himself? How does he depart? How does he support the external things and how the physical?'

Atha ha, next; *kausalyaḥ ca āśvalayanaḥ*, Kausalya, the son of Aśvala; *papraccha enam*, asked him, 'Although the greatness of Prāṇa has thus been perceived by the organs which ascertained his true nature, yet he may be an effect, inasmuch as he forms a part of a composite thing. Therefore I ask: *Bhagavan*, O venerable sir; *kutaḥ*, from what source; *eṣaḥ*, this one, Prāṇa, as ascertained; *jāyate*, is born? And being born, *katham*, how, through what special function; does he *āyāti*, come; *asmin śarīre*, to this body? What is the cause of his being embodied? This is the idea. And having entered into the body, *katham*, how; does he *prātiṣṭhate*, dwell (in the body); *pravibhajya ātmānam*, by dividing himself; *kena*, how, through what special function; does he *utkramate*, depart; *asmāt śarīrāt*, from this body? *katham*, how; does he *abhidhatte*, support; the *bāhyam*, external things, in the context of the elements and in the divine context; and how (does he support) *adhyātmam*, in the (individual) physical context?' The verb 'support' has to be supplied.

तस्मै स होवाचातिप्रश्नान् पृच्छसि ब्रह्मिष्ठोऽसीति तस्मा-
त्तेऽहं ब्रवीमि ॥२॥

2. To him he said: You are putting supernormal questions since you are preeminently a knower of Brahman. Hence I speak to you.

Being asked thus, *sah*, he, the teacher; *uvāca ha*, said; *tasmai*, to him: To begin with, Prāṇa himself, being inscrutable, is a subject-matter of intricate questioning. You inquire about the birth etc. even of that Prāṇa. Hence *pṛcchasi*, you ask; *atipraśnān*, supernormal questions;[1] *brahmiṣṭhaḥ asi iti*, for you are preeminently a knower of Brahman.[2] Thereby I am pleased. *Tasmāt*, hence; *aham bravīmi*, I speak; *te*, to you, what you ask for. Listen:

आत्मन एष प्राणो जायते। यथैषा पुरुषे छायैतस्मिन्नेतदा-
ततं मनोकृतेनायात्यस्मिञ्शरीरे ॥३॥

3. From the Self is born this Prāṇa. Just as there can be this shadow when a man is there, so this Prāṇa is fixed on the self. He comes to this body owing to the actions of the mind.

[1] Questions about transcendental verities.

[2] 'You know the supreme Brahman which transcends the inferior Brahman.' This is only by way of encouragement.—A.G.

Ātmanaḥ, from the Self—from the supreme Puruṣa, the Immutable, (or) Reality; *jāyate*, is born; *eṣaḥ*, this Prāṇa spoken of before (Mu.II.i.2-3). Here is an illustration to show how. *Yathā*, as, in the world; there issues *eṣā*, this; *chāyā*, shadow, as an effect; *puruṣe*, when a man, possessed of head, hands, etc. is there as the cause; similarly, *etasmin*, on this, on Brahman, on Puruṣa, on Reality; *ātatam*, is spread, i.e. fixed; *etat*, this one, this principle that is false by nature, is analogous to a shadow, and is called Prāṇa, just as a shadow is linked to a body. He *āyāti*, comes; *asmin śarīre*, to this body; *mano-kṛtena*, owing to the actions of the mind, that is to say, as the result of actions accomplished through the thought or wish of the mind, for the text will say later, 'Virtue results from virtue' etc. (III.7); and there is another Vedic text (on this point): 'Being attached, he, together with the work, attains (that result to which the subtle body or mind is attached)' (Bṛ.IV.iv.6).

यथा सम्राडेवाधिकृतान् विनियुङ्क्ते। एतान् ग्रामानेतान् ग्रामानधितिष्ठस्वेत्येवमेवैष प्राण इतरान् प्राणान् पृथक् पृथगेव संनिधत्ते ॥४॥

4. As it is the king alone who employs the officers saying, 'Rule over these villages, (and) these villages', just so this Prāṇa engages the other organs separately indeed.

In the world, *yathā*, as, in the way in which; *samrāṭ eva*, it is the king alone; who *viniyuṅkte*, employs; *adhikṛtān*, the officers, in the villages etc.—how?—by ordering, '*Adhitiṣṭhasva*, preside over; *etān grāmān*, these villages;

etān grāmān, these villages'; *evam eva*, just so, as is the case in the illustration, so; *prāṇaḥ*, this chief Prāṇa; *saṁnidhatte*, places, engages; *pṛthak pṛthak eva*, separately indeed, in the respective posts; *itarān prāṇān*, the other organs, the eye etc. which are its own manifestations.

पायूपस्थेऽपानं चक्षुःश्रोत्रे मुखनासिकाभ्यां प्राणः स्वयं प्रातिष्ठते मध्ये तु समानः। एष ह्येतद्धुतमन्नं समं नयति तस्मादेताः सप्तार्चिषो भवन्ति ॥५॥

5. He places Apāna in the two lower apertures. Prāṇa himself, issuing out of the mouth and nostrils, resides in the eyes and ears. In the middle, however, is Samāna. Since this one distributes equally all this food that is eaten, therefore these issue out of these seven flames.

To turn now to the divisions. *Pāyupasthe*, in the two lower appertures; he places *apānam*, Apāna, which is a division of himself and which exists engaged in the work of ejecting faeces, urine, etc. So also *prāṇaḥ svayam*, Prāṇa himself, who occupies the place of the sovereign; *prātiṣṭhate*, resides; *cakṣuḥśrotre*, in the eyes and the ears; issuing out *mukha-nāsikābhyām*, through the mouth and nostrils. *Madhye tu*, in the middle, however, in between the places of Prāṇa and Apāna, in the navel; there is *samānaḥ*, Samāna, which is so called because it assimilates all that is eaten or drunk. *Hi*, since; *eṣaḥ*, this one; *nayati samam*, distributes equally (in all parts of the body); *etat hutam annam*, all this that is eaten or drunk, the food that is poured (as a libation) on one's bodily fire; *tasmāt*, therefore; from the burning of what is eaten and drunk, from the fire in the stomach, when it has reached the region of the heart,[1] *bhavanti*, there issue; *etāḥ sapta arciṣaḥ*, these seven flames, that are lodged in the head. The idea is that the revelation of objects like form (or colour) etc. that constitutes what is known as seeing, hearing, etc. is caused by Prāṇa.

हृदि ह्येष आत्मा। अत्रैतदेकशतं नाडीनां तासां शतं शतमेकैकस्यां द्वासप्ततिर्द्वासप्ततिः प्रतिशाखानाडीसहस्राणि भवन्त्यासु व्यानश्चरति ॥६॥

6. This self (i.e. the subtle body) is surely in the heart. There are a hundred and one of the (chief) nerves. Each of them has a hundred (divisions). Each branch is divided into seventy-two thousand sub-branches. Among them moves Vyāna.

Hi eṣaḥ ātmā, this Self—this subtle body associated with the Self—is in fact; *hṛdi*, in the heart, in the space in the heart, which is circumscribed by the lump of flesh shaped like a lotus. *Atra*, in this heart; there are in number, *etat ekaśatam*, this one hundred and one; *nāḍīnām*, of the chief nerves. *Tāsām*, of those chief nerves; *ekaikasyāḥ*, each one has; *śatam śatam*, a hundred divisions. Again, *prati śākhānāḍī-sahasrāṇi*, the thousands of sub-branches into which each of the (one hundred of) branch nerves

[1] The imagery is thus brought out: The digestive power in the stomach is the sacrificial fire; food is the oblation; and sense-knowledge is the flame. The seven organs in the head are: two eyes, two ears, two nostrils, and the mouth. These derive their capacity to act from the energy supplied by food.

is sub-divided are, in each case; *dvāsaptatiḥ*, *dvāsaptatiḥ*, seventy-two, seventy-two. Each of the hundred branches of the main nerves becomes (seventy-two) thousand in number.[1] *Āsu*, among these nerves; *carati*, moves; the vital energy called *vyānaḥ*, Vyāna, the name being derived in the sense of pervasiveness. Vyāna exists wholly pervading the body through the nerves, which like rays from the sun, issue in all directions from the heart. And by becoming particularly active in the joints, shoulders, and vital parts, and in the interim between the functioning of Prāṇa and Apāna, it becomes the performer of deeds requiring strength.

अथैकयोर्ध्व उदानः पुण्येन पुण्यं लोकं नयति पापेन पाप-
मुभाभ्यामेव मनुष्यलोकम् ॥७॥

7. Now then, Udāna, when it is in its upward trend through the one (nerve), leads to a virtuous world as a result of virtue, to a sinful world as a result of sin, and to the human world as a result of both.

Atha, now then; *ekayā*, through that one among those one hundred and one nerves, which proceeds upward and is known as Suṣumnā; the vital force called *udānaḥ*, Udāna, which moves everywhere from the sole of the feet to the head; *ūrdhvaḥ* (*san*), when it has an upward trend; it *nayati*, leads; *puṇyam lokam*, to a virtuous world, such as the world of the gods; *puṇyena karmaṇā*, as a result of deeds

[1] To sum up: There are 101 main nerves; each is divided into one hundred branches; and each of these branches is sub-divided into 72,000 sub-branches. Thus the sub-branches are 727,200,000 and the total number of all nerves is 727,210,201.

that are virtuous, that are enjoined by the scriptures; (it leads) *pāpam*, to a sinful world, to hell, to birth among beasts and so on; *pāpena*, as a result of sin, which is opposed to those (virtuous deeds); (and it leads) *manuṣyalokam*, to the human world; *ubhābhyām eva*, as a result of both virtue and vice, when they predominate equally. The verb 'leads' has to be supplied (everywhere).

आदित्यो ह वै बाह्यः प्राण उदयत्येष ह्येनं चाक्षुषं प्राणमनुगृह्णानः। पृथिव्यां या देवता सैषा पुरुषस्यापानमवष्टभ्यान्तरा यदाकाशः स समानो वायुर्व्यानः ॥८॥

8. The sun is indeed the external Prāṇa. It rises up favouring this Prāṇa in the eye. That deity that is in the earth, favours by attracting Apāna in a human being. The space (i.e. air) that is in the middle, is Samāna. The (common) air is Vyāna.

Ādityaḥ ha vai, it is the well-known sun indeed, in the divine context; that is the *bāhyaḥ prāṇaḥ*, external Prāṇa (i.e. Prāṇa in external manifestation). *Eṣaḥ*, this one, that is such; *udayati*, rises up; it is this one indeed (that rises) *anugṛhṇānaḥ*, favouring; *enam prāṇam*, this Prāṇa; *cākṣuṣam*, that exist in the eye, in the bodily context; that is to say, it favours by vouchsafing light for the eye in the matter of its perception of form. Similarly, *yā devatā pṛthivyām*, the deity that is well known as identified with the earth; *sā eṣā*, that very one, exists by vouchsafing favour; *avaṣṭabhya*, by attracting, keeping under control—by the fact of pulling down; *apānam puruṣasya*, the vital function called Apāna in a human being; this is the idea.

For otherwise the body would fall because of its weight or would fly up into the sky if left free. *Yat* (rather *yaḥ*) *antarā*, that which is in the middle, in the space that exists in between heaven and earth, the air there being referred to by the word space on the analogy of one sitting on a scaffolding;[1] *saḥ*, it, that air; which is *samānaḥ* Samāna—that exists there, helping the vital function called Samāna; this is the idea. For, in common with the air (in the inter-space), Samāna has the similarity of existing in the space within.[2] And *vāyuḥ*, the air in general, that exists externally is Vyāna, because of the similarity of pervasiveness.[3] That is to say, it stays there helping the (vital function called) Vyāna.

तेजो ह वा उदानस्तस्मादुपशान्ततेजाः । पुनर्भवमिन्द्रियैर्मनसि सम्पद्यमानैः ॥९॥

9. That which is well known as luminosity, is Udāna. Therefore, one who gets his light extinguished, attains rebirth together with the organs that enter into (his) mind.

That which is *tejaḥ ha vai*, well known as common[4] luminosity outside; is *udānaḥ*, Udāna, in the body; that is to say, it favours the vital function called Udāna with its

[1] In the sentence, 'The scaffolding is shouting', 'scaffolding' stands for the men sitting on it. Similarly 'space' here stands for the 'air' in space.

[2] *Vāyu* resides in the space between earth and heaven, and Samāna in the space within the body. The point of resemblance is residence within space.

[3] Air pervades the world, and Vyāna pervades the body.

[4] As distinguished from its special manifestation as the sun.

light. Since the agency (viz Udāna) that causes one's leaving the body is of the nature of luminosity, and (while staying in the body) it is favoured by external light, *tasmāt*, therefore; when an ordinary man *upaśāntatejāḥ*, gets his natural light extinguished, then it is to be understood that his life is exhausted and he is about to die. *Saḥ*, he; attains *punarbhavam*, another body (rebirth). How? *Indriyaiḥ*, together with the organs, counting from speech; *sampadyamānaiḥ manasi*, which enter into the mind.

यच्चित्तस्तेनैष प्राणमायाति। प्राणस्तेजसा युक्तः सहात्मना यथासङ्कल्पितं लोकं नयति ॥१०॥

10. Together with whatever thought he had (at the time of death), he enters into Prāṇa. Prāṇa, in association with Udāna and along with the soul, leads him to the world desired by him.

Yaccittaḥ, whatever thought he might have had, at the time of death; *tena*, together with that very thought, and together with the organs; *āyāti prāṇam*, he (the creature) enters into Prāṇa, the chief vital function. The purport is that at the time of death, the activities of the organs having declined, he continues to live only through the functioning of the chief Prāṇa (vital energy). Then the relatives say, 'He breathes', 'He is alive.' That *prāṇaḥ*, Prāṇa, again; *yuktaḥ tejasā*, in association with the function called Udāna; and *saha ātmanā*, along with the soul, the master that enjoys;—that Prāṇa, thus associated only with the function called Udāna—, *nayati*, leads—that enjoyer (of the fruits of work)—, makes him reach, under the influence of virtuous and vicious actions; *lokam yathāsaṁkalpitam*, a world as was desired by him.[1]

य एवं विद्वान् प्राणं वेद न हास्य प्रजा हीयतेऽमृतो भवति तदेष: श्लोक: ॥११॥

11. The line of progeny of any man of knowledge who knows Prāṇa thus, certainly sustains no break. He becomes immortal. Pertaining to this there occurs this *mantra*.

Yaḥ vidvān, any illumined man who; *veda*, knows; *prāṇam*, Prāṇa; *evam*, thus, as possessed of the descriptions set forth before, viz origin etc.; for that man is being stated this result accruing in this world and the next. *Asya*, for him, for that man of knowledge; *prajāḥ*, line of progeny consisting of sons, grandsons, etc.; *na ha hīyate*, certainly sustains no break. And when his body falls, he *bhavati*, becomes; *amṛtaḥ*, immortal, through his identity with Prāṇa. *Tat*, pertaining to this idea; *bhavati*, there occurs; *eṣaḥ ślokaḥ*, this *mantra*, in the form of brief statement expressive of this idea:

उत्पत्तिमायतिं स्थानं विभुत्वं चैव पञ्चधा ।
अध्यात्मं चैव प्राणस्य विज्ञायामृतमश्नुते
विज्ञायामृतमश्नुत इति ॥१२॥

इति प्रश्नोपनिषदि तृतीय: प्रश्न: ॥

[1] As an aspirant, he had desired heaven etc. when engaged in sacrifices and meditation. That thought becomes again prominent at the time of death and results in the attainment of that very world.

12. Having known the origin, coming, lodgment and fivefold overlordship and the physical existence of Prāṇa, one achieves immortality. Having known, one achieves immortality.

Vijñāya, having known the Prāṇa thus: *utpattim*, the origin of Prāṇa, from the supreme Self (III.3); *āyatim*, (his) coming to this body, through the actions of the mind (III.3); *sthānam*, (his) lodgment, in such places as the lower apertures (III.5); *ca pañcadhā vibhutvam*, and (his) fivefold overlordship, (his) ordering, like a sovereign, of the different functions of Prāṇa in five ways like a sovereign (III.4); his existence externally in the form of the sun etc., and *adhyātmam*, in the body as the eye etc.;—(one) *aśnute*, achieves; *amṛtam*, immortality. The repetition of '*vijñāya amṛtam aśnute*, having known, he achieves immortality' is by way of concluding the Question.

FOURTH QUESTION

अथ हैनं सौर्यायणी गार्ग्यः पप्रच्छ। भगवन्नेतस्मिन् पुरुषे कानि स्वपन्ति कान्यस्मिञ्जाग्रति कतर एष देवः स्वप्नान् पश्यति कस्यैतत् सुखं भवति कस्मिन्नु सर्वे सम्प्रतिष्ठिता भवन्तीति ॥१॥

1. Then the grandson of Sūrya, born of the family of Garga, asked him, 'O adorable sir, which are the organs that go to sleep in this person? Which keep awake in him? Which is the deity who experiences dream? To whom occurs this happiness? In whom do all get merged?'

Atha, next; *sauryāyaṇī gārgyaḥ*, the grandson of Sūrya, born of the family of Garga; *papraccha ha*, asked; *enam*, this one. All about the impermanent, mundane existence, that relates to manifested things, that is comprised within the domain of lower knowledge (i.e. of ignorance), and that consists of ends and means, have been fully dealt with in the three (previous) Questions; now are begun the succeeding three Questions, since it is necessary to speak about that auspicious, calm, unchanging, immutable Truth which is called Purusa, who cannot be thought of in terms of ends and means, is beyond the vital force, the mind and the senses, exists everywhere internally and externally, and is birthless and the subject-matter of superior knowledge. As to that, the questions are now being raised with a view to stating of what characteristics is that Immutable, from which supreme Immutable, as stated in the second

Muṇḍaka, all objects are born like sparks from a blazing fire, and into which they merge again (Mu.II.i.1); which are all those things that emanate from the Immutable; and how, becoming separated, they merge there itself. *Bhagavan*, O adorable sir; *kāni* (*karaṇāni*), which organs; *asmin puruṣe*, in this person, possessed of head, hands, etc.; *svapanti*, go to sleep, desist from their own functions. And *kāni*, which; *asmin*, in this one; *jāgrati*, keep awake, continue in the state of sleeplessness, go on performing their functions? Among those characterized as body and organs,[1] *kataraḥ eṣaḥ devaḥ*, which is this deity, who; *paśyati svapnān*, experiences dreams? Dream means the perception (of objects) within the body, like those in the waking state, by one who has ceased from the perception of the waking state. The idea is this: Is that activity performed by a deity identified with the effect (viz body or Prāṇa), or by someone identified with the senses (and mind)? *Kasya*, to whom; *bhavati*, occurs; *etat sukham*, this happiness, that is calm (i.e. taintless), effortless (i.e. undisturbed), and unobstructed,[2] and that emerges on the cessation of the activities of the dream and waking states? At that time, *kasmin nu sarve sampratiṣṭhitāḥ bhavanti*, in whom do they all remain completely unified, after desisting from the activities of the dream and waking states? The idea is this: like the juices (collected from various flowers) merging in the honey (of a

[1] *Kārya*, effect, is the body or Prāṇa, and *karaṇāni*, the organs, with the mind at their head. In the reading *kārya-kāraṇāni*, *kāraṇāni*, cause, means the elements from which the body etc. are produced.

[2] *Taintless*, untouched by external objects; *effortless*, expressing itself when all disturbances cease, as does the light of a lamp placed in a windless place; *unobstructed*, unending, it being one with the supreme Bliss.

beehive), or the rivers entering into the sea, they *bhavanti*, become; *sampratiṣṭhitāḥ*, blended without the possibility of being distinguished.[1]

Objection: Since on the analogy of a discarded implement, a scythe for instance, it can be held that the organs desist from their respective duties and rest separately, each in itself, during sleep, therefore, whence can arise in the questioner the surmise that the organs of the sleeping person get merged somewhere?

Answer: The surmise (of the questioner in the text) is quite reasonable. Since in relation to the objects of the waking state the organs (are seen to) stand as a composite whole for the benefit of a master and are not independent, therefore, in consonance with the very fact that composite things are dependent on someone else, it is but reasonable to assume that they become unified in someone even in sleep. Hence this question is quite in keeping with that conjecture. In the present context the question, 'In whom do they all remain completely unified,' is meant to imply, 'Who may he be?'—the question being put by one who wants to know something special about the entity in which all the aggregate of body and organs get merged during sleep and cosmic dissolution.[2]

[1] There are five questions here: The first relates to the perceiver of the waking state. That entity whose cessation from activity leads to dream, must be the actor in the waking state. The second question is, 'Whose function is it to maintain the body in all the three states?' The third relates to the perceiver of the dream; the fourth to the enjoyer of sleep. The fifth asks about the Turīya, the Fourth, the Self, free from the three states of wakefulness, dream, and sleep.

[2] It is the absolute Self that the questioner wants to know, and not the conditioned Self that supports all.

तस्मै स होवाच। यथा गार्ग्य मरीचयोऽर्कस्यास्तं गच्छतः सर्वा एतस्मिंस्तेजोमण्डल एकीभवन्ति। ताः पुनः पुनरुदयतः प्रचरन्त्येवं ह वै तत् सर्वं परे देवे मनस्येकीभवति। तेन तर्ह्येष पुरुषो न शृणोति न पश्यति न जिघ्रति न रसयते न स्पृशते नाभिवदते नादत्ते नानन्दयते न विसृजते नेयायते स्वपितीत्याचक्षते ॥२॥

2. To him he said, O Gārgya, just as all the rays of the setting sun become unified in this orb of light, and they disperse from the sun as it rises up again, similarly all that becomes unified in the high deity, the mind. Hence this person does not then hear, does not see, does not smell, does not taste, does not touch, does not speak, does not grasp, does not enjoy, does not eject, does not move. People say, 'He is sleeping.'

Tasmai, to him; *saḥ*, he, the teacher; *uvāca ha*, said: 'O Gārgya, hear what you asked about. *Yathā*, as; the *marīcayaḥ*, rays; *arkasya*, of the sun; *astam gacchataḥ*, that is setting, becoming invisible; *sarvāḥ*, all, without exception; *ekī-bhavanti*, become unified, inseparable, indistinguishable; *etasmin tejomandale*, in this luminous orb, in this sun that is like a mass of light; *punaḥ*, again; *tāḥ*, they, the rays of that very sun; *udayataḥ punaḥ*, while it is rising again; *pracaranti*, disperse;—as is this illustration—, *evam ha vai*, in a similar way indeed; *sarvam tat*; all that, all the senses and their objects; *ekī-bhavati*, become unified; *pare deve manasi*, in the high deity, in the fully luminous mind—since the deities of the eye etc. are dependent on (that of) the mind, the latter is their high deity; in that (mind) they become united, lose their distinction, during dream (and sleep), like the rays in the solar orb. And when a man is about to wake up, they emanate—they proceed to their respective functions—from the mind itself just like the rays radiating from the orb. Since the ears etc., which are the organs of perception of sound etc., desist from their function as organs, and thus seem to be unified in the mind,[1] *tena*, therefore; *tarhi*, at that time, during the time of sleep; *eṣaḥ puruṣaḥ*, this person—to wit, a person named Devadatta; *na śṛṇoti*, does not hear; *na paśyati*, does not see; *na jighrati*, does not smell; *na rasayate*, does not taste; *na spṛśate*, does not touch; *na abhivadate*, does not converse; *na ādatte*, does not grasp; *na ānandayate*, does not enjoy; *na visṛjate*, does not eject; *na iyāyate*, does not move; *ācakṣate*, they, the common people, say: *svapiti iti*, he is asleep.

प्राणाग्नय एवैतस्मिन् पुरे जाग्रति। गार्हपत्यो ह वा एषोऽपानो व्यानोऽन्वाहार्यपचनो यद्गार्हपत्यात् प्रणीयते प्रणयनादाहवनीयः प्राणः ॥३॥

3. It is the fires (i.e. the functions resembling fire) of Prāṇa that really keep awake in this city of the body. That which is this Apāna really resembles the Gārhapatya, Vyāna resembles the Anvāhāryapacana. Since the Āhavanīya is obtained from Gārhapatya which is the (former's)

[1] The senses cannot actually become identified with the mind, since the mind is not their material cause. They simply give up their activities and continue to exist in their dependence on the mind.

source of extraction, therefore Prāṇa conforms to Āhavanīya (because of its issuing out of Apāna[1]).

When the organs, such as the ear, sleep *etasmin pure*, in this city of the body, which is possessed of nine gates; *prāṇāgnayaḥ*, the five divisions of the vital function counting from Prāṇa, which are comparable to fires; *jāgrati*, keep awake. The resemblance with fire is being stated: *Eṣaḥ apānaḥ ha vai gārhapatyaḥ*, this Apāna is really (the sacrificial fire called) Gārhapatya. How that can be so is being stated: Since the other fire called Āhavanīya is *praṇīyate*, obtained (extracted)—at the time of the Agnihotra sacrifice—; *gārhapatyāt praṇayanāt*, from the Gārhapatya fire which is the (former's) source of extraction, therefore, from the derivative sense of 'that from which something is taken away', Gārhapatya fire is the *praṇayana*, the source of extraction. Similarly, for a man in sleep, Prāṇa moves through the mouth and nostrils, having been extracted, as it were, from the function called Apāna. Therefore Prāṇa is comparable to Āhavaṇīya. As for *vyānaḥ*, Vyāna, since it moves out from heart through the *dakṣiṇa*, right, orifice, and is thus associated with the *dakṣiṇa*, southern direction, therefore it is (the fire called) Dakṣiṇāgni, known otherwise as Anvāhāryapacana.

यदुच्छ्वासनिःश्वासावेतावाहुती समं नयतीति स समानः। मनो ह वाव यजमानः। इष्टफलमेवोदानः। स एनं यजमान-महरहर्ब्रह्म गमयति ॥४॥

[1] Apāna draws in the breath and fills up the lungs; from that inner air Prāṇa comes out as the outgoing breath.

4. That Samāna (is the priest called Hotā), because it strikes a balance between exhalation and inhalation which are but (comparable to) two oblations. The mind is verily the sacrificer. The desired fruit is Udāna, which leads this sacrificer every day to Brahman.

The two oblations consisting of *ucchvāsa-niḥśvāsau*, exhaling and inhaling; are the *āhutī*, two oblations, of the Agnihotra sacrifice, as it were, just because of the similarity of being two in number. *Yat*, since—since these are oblations; and since that vital function (called Samāna) *samam nayati*, strikes a balance, for ever; between *etau āhutī*, these two oblations, so as to ensure the maintenance of the body; *iti*, therefore, it is here verily the priest called the Hotā, because of the similarity of carrying the oblations (like the priest), and this despite the fact that it is called a fire (in the earlier paragraph). Which is it? *Saḥ samānaḥ*, it is Samāna. And therefore, the sleep of an illumined man is verily a performance of the Agnihotra sacrifice. Therefore the idea implied is that the illumined man is not to be considered a non-performer of rites. It is thus that in the Vājasaneyaka it is said that all the component parts of the body and organs of this illumined man perform sacrifices at all times even while he sleeps.[1] Such being the case,

[1] By the text, '*Vāk citaḥ, prāṇaḥ citaḥ, cakṣuḥ citaḥ,*' etc. in the Vājasaneyaka, it is enjoined that one should think of the activity of each function of the Prāṇa as a performance of sacrifice. And so it is pointed out that the organs of knowledge and action continue their sacrifices even during the sleep of a man who knows thus. The text there is meant as a praise of this knowledge. Similarly, in the present context the purpose is not to enjoin a meditation, it being out of place under this topic of transcendental knowledge, but to eulogise illumination.

manaḥ ha vāva yajamānaḥ, it is the mind that is the sacrificer, which keeps awake after having poured (as oblation) the external organs and their objects into the wakeful fires of Prāṇa, and which seeks to reach Brahman, like (an actual *yajamāna*, sacrificer, seeking to reach) heaven which is the result of Agnihotra. The mind is imagined to be the sacrificer, because, like the sacrificer, it acts as the chief among the aggregate of body and senses, and because it sets out for Brahman, just as the sacrificer does for heaven. *Iṣṭaphalam eva*, the result itself of the sacrifice; is *udānaḥ*, the vital function called Udāna, because the achievement of the result of a sacrifice depends on Udāna. How? *Saḥ*, he, Udāna; *ahaḥ ahaḥ*, every day; *gamayati*, leads; *yajamānam*, the sacrificer, called the mind; to *brahma*, Brahman, the Immutable, as though to heaven, during the time of sleep, after causing the mind to cease even from the dream activities. Hence Udāna takes the place of the result of the sacrifice.

Thus is praised the illumination of the enlightened man by showing that, starting from the time of cessation from activity of the ear etc., till the time that he rises up from sleep, he enjoys the fruit of all sacrifices, and his sleep is not a source of evil as it is in the case of an unenlightened man; (and all this is meant as a praise), for (on a contrary view) it cannot be held that in the enlightened man alone the ears etc. sleep, or that the fires of the Prāṇas keep awake, or that (only) his mind alone enjoys freedom in the dream and wakeful states and then goes to sleep every day; for the fact of passing through the three states of waking, dream, and sleep is similar for all creatures. Hence it is reasonable to say that this is only a eulogy of enlightenment. As for the question, 'Which is the deity who experiences dream?', that is being answered:

अत्रैष देवः स्वप्ने महिमानमनुभवति। यद्दृष्टं दृष्टमनु-
पश्यति श्रुतं श्रुतमेवार्थमनुशृणोति देशदिगन्तरैश्च प्रत्यनुभूतं
पुनः पुनः प्रत्यनुभवति दृष्टं चादृष्टं च श्रुतं चाश्रुतं चानुभूतं
चाननुभूतं च सच्चासच्च सर्वं पश्यति सर्वः पश्यति ॥५॥

5. In this dream state this deity (i.e. the mind) experiences greatness. Whatever was seen, it sees again; whatever was heard, it hears again; whatever was perceived in the different places and directions, it experiences again and again; it perceives all by becoming all that was seen or not seen, heard or not heard, perceived or not perceived, and whatever is real or unreal.

Atra svapne, in this state of dream, when the organs, such as that of hearing, cease to function, and the vital forces, counting from Prāṇa, keep awake for the maintenance of the body—in this intermediate state (between waking and sleep) before entering into deep sleep; *eṣaḥ devaḥ*, this deity (the mind), that has withdrawn into itself all the organs such as the ear, like the rays of the setting sun; *anubhavati*, experiences, attains; *mahimānam*, greatness, consisting in assuming diverse forms of subject and object.

Objection: The mind is an instrument of the perceiver in the matter of experiencing greatness. Hence, how is it said that the mind experiences independently? It is, indeed, the soul, (conscious of the body), that can be free (in dream).

Answer: That is no defect, for that freedom of the soul is a result of its being conditioned by the mind, inasmuch as the soul by itself does not in reality either dream or keep wake. That its wakefulness and dream are caused by the limiting adjunct of the mind has been stated in the (following text of the) Vājasaneyaka Upaniṣad: 'Being associated with the mind, and being identified with dream', 'it (i.e. the soul) thinks, as it were, and it shakes, as it were', etc. (Bṛ.IV.iii.7). Therefore it is quite logical to speak of the independence of the mind in the matter of experiencing diverse manifestations. Some assert that if the soul is conditioned by the mind in dream, its self-luminosity[1] will remain unestablished. (But) that is not so. That is a false notion of theirs, caused by non-comprehension of the drift of the Upaniṣads, inasmuch as even all such talk about the Self—starting with (the texts dealing with) self-luminosity and ending with emancipation—is within the range of ignorance. It is caused by such conditioning factors as the mind. And this conclusion is arrived at according to such Vedic text as: 'When there is something else, as it were, then one can see something. . . .' (Bṛ.IV. iii.31); 'For him there is no contact with sense-objects'; 'But when to the knower of Brahman everything has become the Self, then what should one see and through what?' (Bṛ.II.iv.14). Accordingly, this doubt arises only in those

[1] As shown in Bṛhadāraṇyaka, IV.iii.14: 'When he dreams, he takes away a little of the impressions of this all-embracing world (the waking state), he himself puts the body aside and himself creates (a dream body) revealing his own lustre by his own light. . . . In this state he becomes self-effulgent.' If the Self continues to be conditioned by the mind in dream, one may well suspect that the effulgence of knowledge revealed there does not belong to the Self.

who have imperfect knowledge of Brahman, but not in those who have realized the non-dual Self.

Objection: If such be the explanation, the specific statement, 'In this state (i.e. dream) he becomes self-effulgent' (Bṛ.IV.iii.9), becomes meaningless.

The *answer* to this is being given: This objection of yours falls far short of your mark, since the self-effulgence will be much more meaningless if the Self is (really) delimited within the heart according to the Vedic text, 'lies in the Space[1] that is within the heart' (Bṛ.II.i.17).

Objection: Though, as a matter of fact, this defect does arise from that point of view, yet half the weight (of this defect) is removed in dream by the fact that the Self becomes then self-effulgent in Its isolation (i.e. dissociation from the mind).[2]

Answer: Not so; for even there (in sleep), persists the association (of the Self) with the nerves extending up to the pericardium (i.e. the whole body) in accordance with the Vedic text, '(When it becomes fast asleep, . . . it comes back along the seventy-two thousand nerves, called Hitā, which extend from the heart to the pericardium), and sleeps (i.e. remains) in the body' (Bṛ.II.i.19); and therefore it is a vain intention to remove the (remaining) half weight even in sleep through your reliance on the argument of the self-effulgence of the person.

Objection: What then is meant by saying that 'the person becomes self-effulgent in this state' (Bṛ. IV. iii. 9)?

[1] The 'Space' (*ākāśa*) here stands really for the supreme Self; but a literal interpretation leads us astray.

[2] The remaining defect will be removed in the state of sleep, where the Self alone exists—this is the implied idea.

Pseudo-Vedāntin: That Vedic text has no application here, since it belongs to a different branch (of the Vedas).

Objection: Not so, since it is desirable that the Vedic texts should all lead to an identical conclusion, for it is the one Self that is the subject-matter of the Upaniṣads and that is sought to be taught and understood. Hence it is necessary that the self-effulgence of the Self in dream should be upheld, for the Vedas serve to reveal the real truth.

Vedāntin: In that case, hear the purport of the Vedic passage by giving up all conceit, for not through conceit can the meaning of the Vedas be mastered even in a hundred years by all the people who pose to be learned. As the Self, sleeping in the space within the heart and in the nerves, spreading from the heart to the pericardium, can be shown to be distinct from them just because It has no (natural) association with them, and thus the Self's self-effulgence does not become negated, similarly, although the mind persists (in dream), together with the impressions activated by ignorance, desire, and past actions, yet the most arrogant sophist cannot deny then the self-effulgence of the Self which, while remaining totally dissociated from the entire group of body and organs, witnesses through ignorance the mental impressions created by past actions like something different from Itself; for the witnessing Self(then) remains distinct from the impressions that form the objects visualized (by It). Hence it has been well said that when the organs merge into the mind which, however, remains unabsorbed, (the Self,) as identified with the mind, sees dreams.

How the mind experiences its diverse manifestations is being said: Being under the influence of the impressions of any object—be it of a friend or of a son etc.—*yat*, which;

dṛṣṭam pūrvam, was seen earlier; it *paśyati*, sees; it seems to think through ignorance that it sees the vision resembling the son or the friend, called up by those impressions of the son, friend, etc. So also, *śrutam artham*, whatever was heard; *anuśṛṇoti*, it seems to hear thereafter, under the influence of its impressions. Similarly, whatever was *pratyanubhūtam deśadigantaraiḥ*, perceived as belonging to the different places and quarters; it *pratyanubhavati*, experiences, appears to experience, through ignorance; *punaḥ punaḥ*, time and again. So also whatever was *dṛṣṭam*, seen, in this birth; and *adṛṣṭam*, not seen, that is to say, seen in another birth; for no impression can be left by what is absolutely unseen. Similarly, with regard to *śrutam ca aśrutam ca*, whatever was heard and not heard; *anubhūtam*, what was perceived, in this life through the mind alone; *ananubhūtam ca*, and whatever was not perceived, that is to say, was perceived by the mind itself in another birth; *ca sat*, and what is true, for instance the real water etc.; *ca asat*, and what is false, for instance, water in a mirage etc. To be brief, it *paśyati*, sees; *sarvam*, all, enumerated or not; *sarvaḥ* (*san*), by becoming all, by becoming conditioned by all the mental impressions. Thus the deity, the mind, sees the dreams in its unification with all the organs.

स यदा तेजसाऽभिभूतो भवति। अत्रैष देवः स्वप्नान्न पश्यत्यथ तदैतस्मिञ्शरीर एतत्सुखं भवति ॥६॥

6. When that deity, (the mind,) becomes overwhelmed by (the solar) rays (called bile), then in this state the deity does not see dreams. Then, at that time, threre occurs this happiness in this body.

Yādā, when, at the time when; *tejasā*, by the light, by the solar light, called bile[1], that is lodged in the nerves; *saḥ*, the deity, called mind; *bhavati*, becomes; completely *abhibhūtaḥ*, overwhelmed—when the doors[2] for its tendencies are closed down; then the rays of the mind, together with the organs, get collected in the heart. The mind is in sleep when, like fire in wood, it exists in the body, pervading it as a whole, in the form of general (as opposed to particularized) consciousness. *Atra*, at this time; *esaḥ*, this; *devaḥ*, deity (lit. the luminous one), called the mind; *na paśyati svapnān*, does not see dreams, the doors of vision having been closed by the light. *Atha tadā*, then at that time; *etasmin śarīre*, in this body; *bhavati*, occurs; *etat sukham*, this happiness that is of the nature of unobstructed Consciousness; that is to say, Bliss then pervades the whole body in a general way and it remains undisturbed.

At this time, the body and organs that depend on ignorance, desire, and the result of past actions, become inactive. When these become quiet, the nature of the Self, that appears distorted owing to the limiting adjuncts, becomes non-dual, one, auspicious, and calm. In order to indicate this state through a process of (successively) merging into it the subtle forms of earth etc. that are creations of ignorance, the text cites an illustration:

स यथा सोम्य वयांसि वासोवृक्षं संप्रतिष्ठन्ते। एवं ह वै तत् सर्वं पर आत्मनि संप्रतिष्ठते ॥७॥

[1] As also by the Consciousness, called Brahman, where the mind merges.

[2] Impressions of past actions that can produce dream.

7. To illustrate the point: As the birds, O goodlooking one, proceed towards the tree that provides lodging, just so all these proceed to the supreme Self.

Saḥ, that illustration, is this: *Yathā*, as; *somya*, O good-looking one; *vayāṁsi*, birds; *sampratiṣṭhante*, proceed towards; *vāsovṛkṣam*, the tree that provides lodging; *evam ha vai*, just so, just as it is in the illustration; *sarvam*, all—that will be enumerated; *sampratiṣṭhate*, proceeds; *pare ātmani*, to the supreme Self, to the Immutable.

पृथिवी च पृथिवीमात्रा चाऽऽपश्चाऽऽपोमात्रा च तेजश्च तेजोमात्रा च वायुश्च वायुमात्रा चाऽऽकाशश्चाऽऽकाशमात्रा च चक्षुश्च द्रष्टव्यं च श्रोत्रं च श्रोतव्यं च घ्राणं च घ्रातव्यं च रसश्च रसयितव्यं च त्वक्च स्पर्शयितव्यं च वाक्च वक्तव्यं च हस्तौ चाऽऽदातव्यं चोपस्थश्चानन्दयितव्यं च पायुश्च विसर्जयितव्यं च पादौ च गन्तव्यं च मनश्च मन्तव्यं च बुद्धिश्च बोद्धव्यं चाहंकारश्चाहंकर्तव्यं च चित्तं च चेतयितव्यं च तेजश्च विद्योतयितव्यं च प्राणश्च विधारयितव्यं च ॥८॥

8. Earth and the rudiment of earth, water and the rudiment of water, fire and the rudiment of fire, air and the rudiment of air, space and the rudiment of space, the organ and object of vision, the organ and object of hearing, the organ and object of smell, the organ and object of taste, the organ and object of touch, the organ and content of speech, the hands and the object grasped, sex and enjoyment, the organ of excretion and the excreta, the feet and the space trodden, the mind and the content of thought,

understanding and the content of understanding, egoism and the content of egoism, awareness and the content of awareness, the shining skin and the object revealed by that, Prāṇa and all that has to be held by Prāṇa.

What are all those things? *Pṛthivī*, the gross earth, possessed of the five attributes;[1] *ca*, and; its cause, the *pṛthivī-mātrā*, rudiment of earth, the fine form of smell. Similarly *āpaḥ ca āpo-mātrā ca*, water and the rudiment of water; *tejaḥ ca tejo-mātrā ca*, fire and the rudiment of fire; *vāyuḥ ca vāyu-mātrā ca*, air and the rudiment of air; *ākāśaḥ ca ākāśa-mātrā ca*, space and the rudiment of space. That is to say, all the gross and subtle elements. So also *cakṣuḥ*, eye, the organ; *ca rūpam*, and the object of sight; *śrotram ca śrotavyam ca*, ear and the object of hearing; *ghrāṇam ca ghrātavyam ca*, the organ and the object of smell; *rasaḥ ca rasayitavyam ca*, the organ and the object of taste; *tvak ca sparśayitavyam ca*, the organ and the object of touch; *vāk ca vaktavyam ca*, speech and the content of speech; *hastau ca ādātavyam ca*, the two hands and the objects to be grasped; *upasthaḥ ca ānandayitavyam ca*, sex and what is enjoyed; *pāyuḥ ca visarjayitavyam ca*, the organ of excretion and what is excreted; *pādau ca gantavyam ca*, the two feet and the place walked over. Thus (it is to be understood) that the organs of knowledge and the organs of action have been enumerated. *Manaḥ ca*, the mind, that has been already mentioned; *mantavyam ca*, and the object of the

[1] Sound, touch, colour, taste, and smell, the last one being the essential attribute of earth. The four others are the essential qualities of space, air, fire and water respectively. These rudimentary elements combine to form the gross composite elements, their names being given according to the predominance of one or the other.

mind (what is thought of); *buddhiḥ*, understanding, the faculty of ascertaining; *ca boddhavyam*, and the object to be ascertained. *Ahaṁkāraḥ*, the internal organ characterized by egoism; *ca*, and; *ahaṁkartavyam*, the object of egoism. *Cittam*, the internal organ possessed of consciousness; *ca cetayitavyam*, and the object to be conscious of. *Tejaḥ*, the skin—as distinct from the organ of touch, and possessed of lustre; the object[1] revealed by it is *vidyotayitavyam*. *Prāṇaḥ* is what is called Sūtra (Hiraṇyagarbha, who strings together everything); *vidhārayitavyam*, is all that is held, strung together by Him. (All these merge in the supreme Self) for, the entire range of body and organs, combining for the sake of some one else and consisting of name and form, extends thus far only.

Next in order is that reality of the Self that has entered here (in the body)—like a reflection of the sun in water, etc.—as the enjoyer and the agent of action.

एष हि द्रष्टा स्प्रष्टा श्रोता घ्राता रसयिता मन्ता बोद्धा कर्ता विज्ञानात्मा पुरुषः । स परेऽक्षर आत्मनि संप्रतिष्ठते ॥९॥

9. And this one is the seer, feeler, hearer, smeller, taster, thinker, ascertainer, doer—the Puruṣa (pervading the body and organs), who is a knower by nature. He becomes wholly established in the supreme, immutable Self.

Hi, and;[2] *eṣaḥ*, this one (this Self); is the *draṣṭā*, seer; *spraṣṭā*, toucher (feeler); *śrotā*, hearer; *ghrātā*, smeller;

[1] I.e. the skin itself that is the seat of the organ of touch.

[2] According to A.G.

rasayitā, taster; *mantā*, thinker; *boddhā*, ascertainer; *kartā*, doer. The word *vijñāna*, when derived in the (instrumental) sense of 'that by which anything is known', means such instruments as the intellect; but the word here is derived in the nominative sense of 'that which knows'. So *vijñānātmā* means the reality which has that nature or which is a knower by nature. He is *puruṣaḥ*, because he fills up, in its entirety, the aggregate of the body and organs that has been spoken of as a limiting adjunct. And as the reflections —of the sun in water, etc.—enters into the sun etc. (when the water etc. is removed), so this Self gets wholly established *pare akṣare ātmani*, in the supreme immutable Self, which persists as the last resort of the universe.

The result achieved by one who realizes his identity with that supreme Self is being stated:

परमेवाक्षरं प्रतिपद्यते स यो ह वै तदच्छायमशरीरमलोहितं शुभ्रमक्षरं वेदयते यस्तु सोम्य। स सर्वज्ञः सर्वो भवति। तदेष श्लोकः ॥१०॥

10. He who realizes that shadowless, bodiless, colourless, pure, Immutable attains the supreme Immutable Itself. O amiable one, he, again, who realizes,[1] becomes omniscient and all. Illustrative of this there occurs this verse:

It is being stated that he *pratipadyate*, attains; *param eva akṣaram*, the supreme Immutable Itself, which has

[1] This translation follows A.G.

the characteristics going to be stated. *Saḥ*, he; (attains the Immutable); *yaḥ ha vai*, who perchance, having become free from all desires; *vedayate*, realizes; *tat*, that which is; *acchāyam*, free from shadow, from ignorance; *aśarīram*, bodiless, devoid of a body conditioned by all the limiting adjuncts constituted by name and form; *alohitam*, devoid of redness, free from all such qualities as redness. Since this is so, therefore (It is) *śubhram*, pure; being free from all attributes. It is *akṣaram*, the immutable, the True, called Puruṣa (the all-pervading, indwelling Entity)—without Prāṇa, not conceivable by the mind, auspicious, calm, coexisting with all that is within and without, and birthless. *Tu*, again; *somya*, O amiable one; *yaḥ*, he, the renouncer of everything, who knows, becomes *sarvajñaḥ*, omniscient; nothing can possibly remain unknown to him. Formerly he was not omniscient owing to ignorance; again, when ignorance is removed by knowledge, *saḥ bhavati sarvaḥ*, he becomes all. *Tat*, with regard to that point; *bhavati eṣaḥ ślokaḥ*, there occurs this verse, which sums up the above idea.

विज्ञानात्मा सह देवैश्च सर्वैः
प्राणा भूतानि संप्रतिष्ठन्ति यत्र।
तदक्षरं वेदयते यस्तु सोम्य
स सर्वज्ञः सर्वमेवाविवेशेति ॥११॥

इति प्रश्नोपनिषदि चतुर्थः प्रश्नः ॥

11. O amiable one, he who knows that Immutable into which the cognizing Self—(the Puruṣa who is naturally a knower)—as also the organs and the elements together

with all the deities merge, that omniscient one enters into everything.

Somya, O amiable (or good-looking) one; *yaḥ tu vedayate*, he who knows; *tat akṣaram*, that Immutable; *yatra*, into which; *vijñānātmā*, the entity that is by nature a knower (IV.9); and *prāṇāḥ*, the organs, such as the eye; *bhūtāni*, and the elements such as earth; *saha devaiḥ*, together with the deities, such as Fire etc.; *saṁpratiṣṭhanti*, merge; *saḥ sarvajñaḥ*, that omniscient one; *āviveśa* (is the same as *āviśati*) enters; into *sarvam*, everything.

FIFTH QUESTION

अथ हैनं शैब्यः सत्यकामः पप्रच्छ। स यो ह वै तद्भग-
वन्मनुष्येषु प्रायणान्तमोंकारमभिध्यायीत। कतमं वाव स तेन
लोकं जयतीति। तस्मै स होवाच ॥१॥

1. Next, Satyakāma, son of Śibi, asked him, 'O venerable sir, which world does he really win thereby, who among men, intently meditates on *Om* in that wonderful way till death?' To him he said:

Atha ha, next; *satyakāmaḥ śaibyaḥ*, Satyakāma, son of Śibi; *papraccha enam*, asked him. Now then, this Question is begun in order to enjoin the meditation on *Om* as a means to the realization of the inferior and the superior Brahman. *Bhagavan*, O venerable sir; *saḥ yaḥ ha vai*, anyone, any rare person; *manuṣyeṣu*, among men; who, after withdrawing the organs from external objects and concentrating his mind on *Om*, on which he superimposes the idea of Brahman through devotion; *abhidhyāyīta*, should intently meditate; *oṁkāram*, on *Om*; *tat*, in that wonderful way; *prāyaṇāntam*, till death, that is to say, for the whole life; (which world does he conquer)? The meaning of the term '*abhidhyāna*, intense meditation', is to have such an unbroken current of the idea of self-identification (with the object of meditation) as is not vitiated by other states of consciousness of a different order, and which is comparable to the (unflickering) flame of a lamp in a windless place. There being many worlds that can be achieved through meditation and rites, *katamam vāva lokam*, which of the worlds; *saḥ jayati tena*, does he conquer thereby, by that meditation on *Om*, who undertakes such a lifelong vow, aided by such multifarious forms of *yama* and *niyama* (i.e. control of body and organs, and observance of moral injunctions) as truthfulness, abstinence from sexual pleasure, noninjury, non-acceptance of presents, dispassion, monasticism, cleanliness, contentment, absence of dissimulation, etc.? To him who had asked thus, *saḥ*, he, Pippalāda; *uvāca ha*, said:

एतद्वै सत्यकाम परं चापरं च ब्रह्म यदोंकारः।
तस्माद्विद्वानेतेनैवाऽऽयतनेनैकतरमन्वेति ॥२॥

2. O Satyakāma, this very Brahman, that is (known as) the inferior and superior, is but this *Om*. Therefore the illumined soul attains either of the two through this one means alone.

O Satyakāma; *etat brahma vai*, this very Brahman; *yat*, that is; *param ca aparam ca*, both superior and inferior—the superior being that which is Truth and Immutable and is called Puruṣa, and the inferior being the First Born, called Prāṇa; *oṁkāraḥ eva*, is but *Om*, is identical with *Om*, since *Om* is Its symbol.[1] As the supreme Brahman cannot be (directly) indicated by words etc. and is devoid of all distinctions created by attributes—and as It is (on that account) beyond the organs—therefore the mind by itself cannot explore It. But to those who meditate on *Om*, which is comparable to the images of Viṣṇu and

[1] *Etat* and *yat*, being neuter, are construed with Brahman, rather than with *oṁkāraḥ* which is masculine.—A.G.

others and on which is fixed the idea of Brahman with devotion, that Brahman becomes favourable (and reveals Itself). This is understood on the authority of scriptures. Similar is the case with the inferior Brahman. Hence it is said in a secondary sense that, that Brahman which is both inferior and superior is but *Om*. *Tasmāt*, therefore; *vidvān*, one who knows, thus; *anveti*, attains; *ekataram*, either of the two—the superior or the inferior Brahman; *etena āyatanena eva*, through this means alone, through this that is a means for the attainment of the Self, consisting in meditation on *Om*; for *Om* is the nearest symbol of Brahman.

स यद्येकमात्रमभिध्यायीत स तेनैव संवेदितस्तूर्णमेव जगत्यामभिसंपद्यते। तमृचो मनुष्यलोकमुपनयन्ते स तत्र तपसा ब्रह्मचर्येण श्रद्धया संपन्नो महिमानमनुभवति ॥३॥

3. Should he meditate on *Om* as consisting of one letter he becomes enlightened even by that and very quickly attains a human birth on the earth. The *Rk mantras* lead him to the human birth. Being endued there with self-control, continence and faith he experiences greatness.

Yadi, even though; *saḥ*, he; may not know all the letters by which *Om* is constituted, still through the influence of the (partial) meditation on *Om*, he attains an excellent goal; one who resorts to *Om* does not fall into evil by being denied the fruits of both rites and meditation as a consequence of the defect of such partial knowledge. What ensues then? Being merely a knower of only one part consisting of one letter, *abhidhyāyīta*, should he thus meditate, constantly; on *Om* itself as comprising one letter; *saḥ*, he; *saṁveditaḥ*, becoming enlightened; *tena eva*, by that alone — by that meditation on *Om* as possessed of one letter only; *tūrṇam eva*, very quickly; *abhi-saṁpadyate*, attains; *jagatyām*, on the earth. What does he attain? *Manuṣyalokam*, the human birth (i.e. human body). As many kinds of birth are possible on this earth, so, among these, *ṛcaḥ*, the *Ṛk mantras*; *upanayante*, conduct; *tam*, him, that aspirant; to *manuṣyalokam*, a human birth, on the earth; for the first single letter (viz *a*) of *Om* was meditated on (by him) as the *Ṛk mantras*, which stand for the Ṛg-veda. Thereby, in that human birth, he becomes a prominent Brāhmaṇa, and being *saṁpannaḥ*, endued; *tapasā*, with self-control; *brahmacaryeṇa*, with continence; *śraddhayā*, with faith; *anubhavati*, experiences; *mahimānam*, greatness; he does not become faithless or wilful in his action. He does not ever come to grief because of any deviation—(consisting in partial knowledge)—from Yoga (i.e. application of his mind to Brahman).

अथ यदि द्विमात्रेण मनसि संपद्यते सोऽन्तरिक्षं यजुर्भि-
रुन्नीयते सोमलोकम्। स सोमलोके विभूतिमनुभूय पुनरावर्तते
॥४॥

4. Now again, if he meditates on *Om* with the help of the second letter (*u*)[1], he becomes identified with the mind. By the *Yajur mantras* he is lifted to the intermediate space, the world of the Moon. Having experienced greatness in the lunar world, he turns round again.

[1] See A.G.

Atha, now again; *yadi*, if, anyone conversant with *Om* as constituted by its second letter (viz *u*); *abhidhyāyīta*, should meditate on *Om*; *dvimātreṇa*, as possessed of the second letter; then as a result of that concentration, one *sampadyate*, becomes unified; *manasi*, in the mind, of which the Moon is the presiding deity, which is conceived of as the state of dream, which is identified with the *Yajur mantras*, and which is the object of meditation. When *saḥ*, that man, who has become thus identified, dies; he is *unnīyate*, lifted; *yajurbhiḥ*, by the *Yajur mantras*, which are verily identical with the second letter; *antarikṣam*, to the intermediate space (between heaven and earth); *somalokam*, to the world of the Moon, which is supported by the intermediate space and is represented by the second letter. That is to say, the *Yajur mantras* lead him to a birth in the world of the Moon. *Saḥ*, he; *anubhūya vibhūtim*, having experienced greatness there; *somaloke*, in the world of the Moon; *āvartate punaḥ*, turns round again, towards the human world.[1]

यः पुनरेतं त्रिमात्रेणोमित्येतेनैवाक्षरेण परं पुरुषमभिध्यायीत स तेजसि सूर्ये संपन्नः। यथा पादोदरस्त्वचा विनिर्मुच्यत एवं ह वै स पाप्मना विनिर्मुक्तः स सामभिरुन्नीयते ब्रह्मलोकं स एतस्माज्जीवघनात् परात्परं पुरिशयं पुरुषमीक्षते। तदेतौ श्लोकौ भवतः ॥५॥

[1] According to Śaṅkarānanda, the first portion of the text means this: If anyone *manasi sampadyate*, resorts to the mind, that is, meditates; *dvimātreṇa*, for two moments or on the two letters *a*, and *u* of *Om*. According to some, this text enjoins a meditation on Hiraṇyagarbha who embodies Himself in the subtle cosmos conceived of as a subtle dream state; the earlier text similarly enjoins a meditation on Virāṭ, embodying Himself in the gross universe, conceived of as the waking state.

5. Again, anyone who meditates on the supreme Puruṣa with the help of this very syllable *Om*, as possessed of three letters, becomes unified in the Sun, consisting of light. As a snake becomes freed from its slough, exactly in a similar way, he becomes freed from sin, and he is lifted up to the world of Brahmā (Hiraṇyagarbha) by the *Sāma mantras*. From this total mass of creatures (that Hiraṇyagarbha is) he sees the Puruṣa who penetrates every being and is higher than the higher One (viz Hiraṇyagarbha). Bearing on this, there occur two verses:

Punaḥ, again; *yaḥ abhidhyāyīta*, should anyone meditate; *etam*, on this—on *Om*; as *param puruṣam*, the supreme Puruṣa, residing within the solar orb; *Om iti etena eva akṣareṇa*, with the help of the very syllable *Om*; *trimātreṇa*, as associated with the knowledge of the three letters (*a, u, m*), and serving as a symbol; (he becomes unified in the Sun) as the result of that meditation. In this context *Om* is (presented as) a symbol to aid (meditation), which conclusion is drawn from the following Vedic text implying identity: 'That which is known as the superior and inferior Brahman (is but *Om*)' (V.2). Moreover, on any other supposition, the frequently used accusative case in *oṁkāram* in the text will become unjustifiable. Although from the use of the instrumental case (in *trimātreṇa*), an interpretation in the instrumental sense is quite in order, still in conformity with the context, *trimātreṇa* etc. should be converted to the accusative form[1] thus: '*trimātram param puruṣam*—(meditate) on *Om*, associated with the knowledge of the three letters, as the supreme Puruṣa', so as to

[1] One might object that the instrumental case indicates that *Om* is not a symbol (or icon); but Śaṅkara says it is so.

accord with the adage, 'The individual should be sacrificed for the family'[1] (Ma.Nā. 37.17). By that meditation, *saḥ*, he; becomes *saṁpannaḥ*, absorbed—being engaged in meditation, he becomes identified with the third letter (*m*) and becomes unified; *tejasi sūrye*, in the sun consisting of light. Even after death he does not return from the Sun as one does from the lunar world; but he continues in his identity with the Sun. *Yathā*, just as; a *pādodaraḥ*, snake; *vinirmucyate tvacā*, is freed from its slough, the dead skin, to become new again; *evam ha vai*, exactly in the same way, as in this illustration, so; becoming *vinirmuktaḥ*, freed; *pāpmanā*, from sin, which is a kind of impurity comparable to the slough; *saḥ*, he; *unnīyate*, is lifted up; *sāmabhiḥ*, by the *Sāma mantras*—that are identical with the third letter (*m* of *Om*); *brahmalokam*, to the world of Brahmā, i.e. of Hiraṇyagarbha, which is called Satya (Truth). That Hiraṇyagarbha is identified with all the creatures that are subject to birth and death; for as (the sum total of all) the subtle bodies, He constitutes the inner soul of all; and in Him, as comprising the (cosmic) subtle body, are strung together all the creatures.[2] Hence He is *jīvaghanaḥ*, a mass of creatures. *Etasmāt jīvaghanāt*, from this totality of creatures, that Hiraṇyagarbha is; *sah*, he, the enlightened man, who has known *Om* as possessed of the three letters; *īkṣate*, sees through meditation; *puruṣam*, Puruṣa; *puriśayam*, who has entered into all the bodies and who is called the supreme Self; being *param parāt*, superior to the higher One, that is to say, to Hiraṇyagarbha.[3] *Tat*, bearing on this

[1] That is to say, for the sake of the majority.

[2] Creatures that identify themselves with their subtle bodies.

[3] Hiraṇyagarbha is higher than all other creatures.

expressive of the foregoing idea; *bhavataḥ*, there occur; *etau ślokau*, these two verses:

तिस्रो मात्रा मृत्युमत्यः प्रयुक्ता
अन्योन्यसक्ता अनविप्रयुक्ताः ।
क्रियासु बाह्याभ्यन्तरमध्यमासु
सम्यक् प्रयुक्तासु न कम्पते ज्ञः ॥६॥

6. The three letters (by themselves) are within the range of death. But if they are closely joined, one to another, are not divergently applied to different objects, and are applied to the three courses of action—external, internal, and intermediate—that are properly resorted to, then the man of enlightenment does not shake (i.e. remains undisturbed).

Tisraḥ mātrāḥ, the three letters, viz *a, u, m*, of *Om*; *mṛtyumatyaḥ*, are encompassed by death, not outside the pale of death, that is to say, surely within the grasp of death.[1] But when they are *prayuktāḥ*, applied; *kriyāsu*, in actions, in the acts of meditation on the Self; and further, (when they are) *anyonyasaktāḥ*, joined one to another; *anaviprayuktāḥ*, are not applied divergently to

[1] Viśva, the conscious Self in the waking state, is identical with Vaiśvānara (Virāṭ), and his residence is in the gross body and the waking state. Taijasa, identical with Hiraṇyagarbha, has his lodging in the subtle body and dream. Prājña, identical with Īśvara, has his locus in the Unmanifested and sleep. The yogic processes consist in meditating on them in identification with *a, u, m*, respectively. If these are resorted to separately, and without the idea of Brahman, they cannot lead one beyond death.

different objects, (then the yogī does not shake). *Viprayuktāḥ* are those that are specifically applied to a single object alone; those that are not applied thus are *aviprayuktāḥ*, (i.e. diversely used); those that are not thus diversely applied are *anaviprayuktāḥ*. What follows from that? When (they are applied thus) specially at the time of a single (continuous) meditation during the three *kriyāsu*, courses of action; *bāhyābhyantaramadhyamāsu*, external, internal, and intermediate—in the course of the yogic actions consisting in the meditation on the Puruṣas as associated with the states of waking, dream, and sleep; *samyak prayuktāsu*, which processes are properly resorted to during the time of meditation; then the *jñaḥ*, enlightened one, that is to say, the yogī who knows the aforesaid divisions of *Om*; *na kampate*, does not shake. He who knows thus, cannot possibly be deflected, since the Puruṣas in the waking, dream, and sleep states, together with the states, have been seen by him as identical with the three letters and as identical with *Om*. Since a man who is thus enlightened has become the Self of all and one with *Om*, therefore from where can he deviate and to where?

The second verse is meant to sum up all the (foregoing) ideas:

ऋग्भिरेतं यजुर्भिरन्तरिक्षं
सामभिर्यत् तत् कवयो वेदयन्ते ।
तमोंकारेणैवाऽऽयतनेनान्वेति विद्वान्
यत्तच्छान्तमजरममृतमभयं परं चेति ॥७॥

इति प्रश्नोपनिषदि पञ्चमः प्रश्नः ॥

7. The intelligent know this world that is attainable by *Ṛk mantras*, the intermediate space achievable by the *Yajur mantras*, and that which is reached by the *Sāma mantras*. The enlightened man attains that (threefold) world through *Om* alone; and through *Om* as an aid, he reaches that also which is the Supreme (Reality) that is quiet and beyond old age, death, and fear.

Only *kavayaḥ*, the intelligent, the enlightened, and not the ignorant; *vedayante*, know; *etam*, this, this world associated with men; that is attainable *ṛgbhiḥ*, through the *Ṛk mantras*; *antarikṣam*, the intermediate space, presided over by the Moon; that is attainable *yajurbhiḥ*, by the *Yajur mantras*; and *tat*, that, the third, i.e. the world of Brahmā; *yat*, which; is attainable *sāmabhiḥ*, by the *Sāma mantras*. *Vidvān*, the enlightened one; *anveti*, reaches; *tam*, that, that threefold world indicative of the inferior Brahman; *oṁkāreṇa*, through *Om*, with the aid of *Om*. And with the help of that very *Om*, he attains *tat*, that; *yat*, which is the Supreme—Brahman, the Immutable, Truth, called Puruṣa, (the All-pervasive); which is *śāntam*, quiet, free, devoid of all such distinctions as waking, dream, and sleep, and is transcendental to the whole universe; and is therefore *ajaram*, free from old age; *amṛtam*, beyond death, since untouched by such changes as old age; and consequently *abhayam*, fearless; just because It is fearless, therefore *param*, unsurpassing. The idea is that he reaches this One also, *oṁkāreṇa āyatanena*, with the aid of *Om*, which is a vehicle of advance. The word '*iti*, this', is used to imply the end of the sentence.

SIXTH QUESTION

अथ हैनं सुकेशा भारद्वाजः पप्रच्छ। भगवन् हिरण्यनाभः कौसल्यो राजपुत्रो मामुपेत्यैतं प्रश्नमपृच्छत। षोडशकलं भारद्वाज पुरुषं वेत्थ। तमहं कुमारमब्रुवं नाहमिमं वेद। यद्यहमिममवेदिषं कथं ते नावक्ष्यमिति। समूलो वा एष परिशुष्यति योऽनृतमभिवदति तस्मान्नार्हाम्यनृतं वक्तुम्। स तूष्णीं रथमारुह्य प्रवव्राज। तं त्वा पृच्छामि क्वासौ पुरुष इति॥१॥

1. Then Sukeśā, son of Bharadvāja, asked him, 'Venerable sir, Hiranyanābha, a prince of Kosala, approached me and put this question, "Bhāradvāja, do you know the Puruṣa possessed of sixteen limbs?" To that prince I said, "I do not know him. Had I known him, why should I not have told you? Anyone who utters a falsehood dries up root and all. Therefore I cannot afford to utter a falsehood". Silently he went away riding on the chariot. Of that Puruṣa I ask you, Where does He exist?'

Atha ha, next; *sukeśā bhāradvājaḥ*, Sukeśā, son of Bharadvāja; *papraccha*, asked; *enam*, him. It has been said that the entire world, consisting of cause and effect, together with the conscious soul, gets unified in the supreme Immutable during sleep (IV.11). From the logic of circumstances it follows that even during cosmic dissolution, the world merges into that Immutable alone and originates from that alone; for an effect cannot reasonably get absorbed into anything other than its origin. Besides, it has been said, 'From the Self is born this Prāṇa' (III.3). And it is the well ascertained purport of all the Upaniṣads that the highest good results from the full realization of that which is the source of creation; and it has just been declared, 'he becomes omniscient and all' (IV.10). It remains now to point out where that Immutable, that Truth, called Puruṣa (the all-pervasive, indwelling entity) is to be realized. This question is begun for that purpose. And by pointing out the difficulty involved in acquiring the knowledge, the narration of the anecdote aims at inducing a special effort in those who hanker after freedom. *Bhagavan*, O revered sir; a *rājaputraḥ*, prince, Kṣatriya by caste, named Hiraṇyanābha; who was *kausalyaḥ*, born in Kosala; *upetya mām*, approaching me; *apṛcchata*, asked; *etam praśnam*, this question—which is being stated: '*Bhāradvāja*, O son of Bharadvāja; *vettha*, do you know; the *puruṣam*, Puruṣa, (the Reality pervading the body); which is *ṣoḍaśakalam*, possessed of sixteen digits (limbs)?' That conscious Being, the soul, is *ṣoḍaśakalaḥ*, on which, through ignorance, are superimposed sixteen parts that appear like limbs. *Aham*, I; *abruvam*, said; *tam kumāram*, to that prince, who had put the question: '*Aham*, I; *na veda*, do not know; *imam*, this one that you inquire about.' As he thought it impossible that there could be any ignorance in me, despite that statement of mine, I told him as a proof of my ignorance: '*Yadi*, if, perchance; *aham*, I; *avediṣam*, happened to know; *imam*, this one, the Puruṣa inquired about by you; *katham*, why; *na avakṣyam*, should I not have told, that is to say, should not tell you, inquisitive and eminently fitted as a disciple as you are.' Noticing his disbelief over again, I said furthermore to carry conviction to him: '*Yaḥ*, anyone who; *abhivadati*, utters; *anṛtam*, a falsehood, that does not accord with what is—speaks of himself as somewhat other than what he really is; *eṣaḥ*, such a man; *pariśuṣyati*, dries up; *samūlaḥ*, together with roots; he is deprived of this world and the next, he is destroyed. As I know this fact, *tasmāt*, therefore; *na arhāmi anṛtam vaktum*, I cannot afford to utter a falsehood, like an ignoramus.' *Āruhya ratham*, riding on the chariot; *saḥ*, he, the prince, who was thus convinced; *pravavrāja*, went away; to where he had come from; *tūṣṇīm*, silently, with abashment. From this the conclusion is drawn that one who knows must impart knowledge to a disciple who is competent and approaches duly, but one should not utter a falsehood under any condition whatsoever. *Tam puruṣam*, about that Puruṣa—which, as an object still to be ascertained, sticks to my heart like a thorn; *pṛcchāmi tvā*, I ask you; '*Kva asau puruṣaḥ*, where does that Puruṣa (who is to be known) exist?'

तस्मै स होवाच। इहैवान्तःशरीरे सोम्य स पुरुषो यस्मिन्नेताः षोडशकलाः प्रभवन्तीति ॥२॥

2. To him he (Pippalāda) said: O amiable one, here itself inside the body is that Puruṣa in whom originate these sixteen digits (or limbs).

Tasmai, to him; *saḥ*, he; *uvāca ha*, said; *iha eva*, here itself; *antaḥśarīre*, inside the body, within the space inside the lotus of the heart; *somya*, O amiable one; exists *saḥ puruṣaḥ*, that Puruṣa—and He is not to be sought somewhere else—; *yasmin*, in whom; *prabhavanti*, originate; *etāḥ ṣoḍaśa-kalāḥ*, these sixteen parts—Prāṇa and the rest that are being enumerated. The Puruṣa who is partless appears through ignorance to be possessed of limbs as a consequence of His association with the sixteen parts that are His limiting adjuncts. But this Puruṣa has to be shown as an absolute entity by eliminating, through knowledge, those parts that condition Him. That is why the parts are spoken of as originating from the Puruṣa. Since no empirical pronouncement as to attainability and the means of attainment can be made unless there be the superimposition of Prāṇa and the rest on the totally attributeless, non-dual, pure principle, therefore, the origin, existence, and absorption of the parts that are within the domain of ignorance, are superimposed (on the Puruṣa); for the parts are always seen to exist in identity with Consciousness at the times of origin, continuation, and dissolution. And this is why some deluded people say, 'Just as ghee (clarified butter) melts through contact with fire, so it is consciousness that originates every moment as pot etc. and gets destroyed.' Others (e.g. the nihilists) say, 'When that consciousness stops, all things appear as void.' Still others (e.g. the logicians) say, 'The knowledge of pot and the rest arises and gets destroyed as a temporary phenomenon on the eternal Self which imparts consciousness.' The materialists say, 'Consciousness belongs to matter.' But Consciousness that knows no decrease or increase, and yet appears diversely through the attributes of the limiting adjuncts, is nothing but the Self, which fact is borne out by such Vedic texts as 'Brahman is truth, knowledge, infinite' (Tai.II.i.1), 'Brahman is Consciousness' (Ai.III.i.3), 'Knowledge, Bliss, Brahman' (Bṛ.III.ix.28.7), 'The infinite Reality is but pure intelligence' (Bṛ.II.iv.12). Consciousness is proved to be invariable from the fact that Consciousness remains unchanged even when objects change in their essence, and because anything that is known in any way, emerges to consciousness only as such an object of knowledge.[1] It does not stand to reason to say that some external thing exists substantially and still remains unknown, for this is like averring that colour is perceived while the eye is non-existent. A knowable thing may be inconstant in relation to knowledge, but knowledge is never inconstant in relation to objects, for knowledge persists in relation to some knowable thing even though a particular object may not be there; indeed, nobody can have such a thing as an object unless he has knowledge.

Objection: Since even consciousness is not perceived in sleep just because it does not exist there then, therefore it follows that knowledge, in itself, is inconstant just like an object.

Answer: No, for in so far as knowledge that reveals its objects is an illuminator of its object just like a light, the absence of knowledge during sleep cannot logically be inferred, just as the absence of light cannot be inferred from the absence of the thing to be lighted up. Certainly, the nihilist cannot imagine the absence of the eye when it fails to perceive colour in darkness.

[1] That things are apprehended to be what they are is owing to the fact of the apparent diversification of the underlying Consciousness by the limiting adjuncts; and things would cease to be known unless Consciousness lay behind them. This proves that things vary, while Consciousness remains unchanged. A pot may not exist even when there is consciousness of it, or objects may vary essentially, while knowledge persists; but there can be no object of knowledge without Consciousness. *Objection*: We have no knowledge of a jar at the time that we know a cloth; so knowledge also is variable. *Answer:* Knowledge may vary as coloured by its objects, but not essentially, whereas things vary essentially.

Objection: The nihilist does, as a matter of fact, imagine the absence of knowledge where there is no knowable thing.

Answer: The nihilist should explain how he would argue away the presence of that knowledge by which he imagines the non-existence of that knowledge; for the non-existence of the knowledge being itself a knowable object, it cannot be cognized unless there is knowledge of it.

Objection: Since knowledge is non-different from the knowable, non-existence of knowledge follows from the non-existence of the knowable object.

Answer: Not so, because non-existence too is admitted as cognizable. By the (Buddhist) nihilist it is admitted that non-existence is also known and that it is everlasting. Now, if knowledge be non-different from (the knowable) non-existence, it also will become eternal *ex hypothesi*; and because the non-existence of knowledge becomes essentially a knowledge, non-existence (of knowledge) is reduced to a meaningless term. In reality, knowledge is neither a non-existence, nor is it non-eternal. Nor do we lose anything if the mere epithet of non-existence is applied to knowledge that is (really) eternal.

If it be now argued that although non-existence is knowable, it is distinct from knowledge, then in that case, the non-existence of the knowable will not lead to the non-existence of knowledge.[1]

[1] By such a theory you nullify your view that knowledge and the knowable are identical. Hence by depending on the assumptions that knowable objects are absent in sleep and that knowledge is non-different from the knowable, you cannot argue that knowledge is non-existent in sleep. Moreover, if the non-existing knowable thing be different from knowledge, why should not an existing knowable thing be different also?

Objection: An object is different from knowledge, but knowledge is not different from its object.

Answer: No, since it is all mere talk that does not lead to any real distinction, for if it be held that object and knowledge are identical, then it is meaningless talk to say that the knowable object is distinct from knowledge, while knowledge is not distinct from its content; and it is comparable to the thesis that *vahni* (fire) is distinct from *agni* (fire), while *agni* is not distinct from *vahni*. If, however, knowledge be different from the content of knowledge, the conclusion arrived at is that the absence of any knowable object does not logically imply the absence of knowledge (as such).

Objection: Since there can be no awareness (of knowledge) when there is no object to be known, it follows that knowledge itself is absent in the absence of any object.

Answer: Not so, for awareness is admitted in sleep inasmuch as it is held by the (Buddhist) nihilists that consciousness persists even in sleep.

Objection: Even there it is held that consciousness is known to itself.

Answer: No, since the distinction of the two (viz knowledge and object) is already postulated. Inasmuch as the knowledge that pertains to an object of the form of non-existence is different from that non-existent object, the difference between the knowable and the knowledge stands as an established fact. That fact having been proved, it cannot be revivified like a dead man, nor can it be reversed by even a hundred nihilistic Buddhists.

Objection: In so far as knowledge is known by some other knowledge, there crops up an infinite regress from your point of view, since that knowledge must have another knowledge to know it, and that again another.

Answer: Not so, for a logical distinction between all (knowledge and objects) is possible. On the admission that everything is knowable to some knowledge, that knowledge which is different from its content remains what it is for ever.[1] This is a second category that is admitted by all who are not nihilists, and no third category to comprehend it is admitted. Thus there is no scope for infinite regress.

Objection: If knowledge remains unknown to itself, then omniscience becomes untenable.

Answer: That defect, too, should affect him (i.e. the Buddhists) alone. What need have we to remove it?[2] Besides, (for him) there is the fault of infinite regress arising from the admission that knowledge is an object of knowledge, for knowledge is certainly knowable according to the (Buddhist) nihilist. And because (a particular) knowledge cannot be known by itself, an infinite regress is inevitable.

Objection: This fault is equally in evidence (in your theory as well).

[1] We hold that things knowable are objects of knowledge, but knowledge itself is not known. The knowable are ever knowable, and so is knowledge ever knowledge.

[2] The Buddhist believes that knowledge is known. So if it can be proved that knowledge is unknowable, omniscience of Buddha, for instance, can no longer be sustained. But the Vedāntin is not open to that charge, as according to him knowledge can cognize only those things that are fit to be known, as otherwise non-omniscience would result from the non-comprehension of such an imaginary thing as the horn of a hare. The Vedāntin may also reply that since the very conception of omniscience is within the domain of ignorance, he is not under any obligation to prove its reality. Or he may argue that omniscience follows from the fact of one's possessing the capacity to know everything that exists, but not necessarily from the actual awareness of everything.

Answer: Not so, for Consciousness (according to us) can logically be shown to be but one. Since it is but one Consciousness, existing in all places, times, persons, etc., that appears diversely because of the differences in the multifarious limiting adjuncts constituted by name, form, etc., just like the reflections of the sun etc. on water etc., therefore that objection has no force; and the statement that is under consideration here agrees with this.[1]

Objection: From the Upaniṣadic text, ('here itself inside the body'—VI.2), it follows that the Puruṣa is contained here inside the body, like a jujube fruit in a vessel.

Answer: No. (this is wrong), because the Puruṣa is the cause of such parts as Prāṇa, and because nobody will understand the Puruṣa as the source of such parts as Prāṇa, faith, etc., if He be delimited by a mere body. And this follows from the further fact that the body is an effect of those parts; because the body, which is constituted by the parts—Prāṇa and the rest, which (in their turn) are the products of the Puruṣa—cannot contain within itself, like a jujube in a vessel, the Puruṣa who is the origin of its own source.

Objection: This is possible on the analogy of the seed and the tree. Just as a tree is the effect of a seed, and the effect of that tree is a fruit, a mango for instance, which holds within itself the (stone that is the) cause of its cause (viz the tree), similarly the body can contain within itself even the Puruṣa, though He is the cause of its own cause (viz Prāṇa etc.).

Answer: This is untenable, because it implies difference and divisibility. In the analogy, the seeds contained in the

[1] On the strength of the fact that Consciousness as an eternal entity is the basis of all appearances, the Upaniṣad talks of the superimposition of the parts (or limbs) on that Consciousness.

fruits of the tree are different from the seed that produced the tree, whereas in the case to which the analogy applies, the very same Puruṣa who is the cause of the causes of the body, is heard of in the Upaniṣad to be confined within the body. Moreover, things like the tree and the seeds can be related by way of the container and the thing contained, because they are composite by nature, whereas the Puruṣa is not divisible, though the parts (viz Prāṇa etc.) and the body are. Hereby it is shown that inasmuch as even space cannot be contained within the body,[1] much less can the Puruṣa, who is the cause of space, be confined within it. Therefore the illustration is inapt.

Objection: Leave alone the analogy. The point is born out by the text itself.

Answer: That cannot be, for texts cannot create things anew, since a text is not meant to reverse anything. What is its function then? It is concerned with expressing things as they are. Therefore the text 'inside the body' is to be understood in the same sense as the statement that space exists within the Cosmic Egg.[2] Besides, that text conforms only to empirical experience in so far as from such logical grounds as (the experiences of) seeing, hearing, thinking, knowing, etc., the Puruṣa is experienced within the body, as though He is a limited being. And since (it is within the body that) He is realized, therefore it is said, 'O amiable one, that Puruṣa is inside the body.' When not even a fool wishes to conceive mentally that the Puruṣa, who is the

[1] *Objection*: The body produced from indivisible space contains space within itself. *Answer*: There too space does not enter into the body, but seems to be existing in the shape of a body as pervading the pores and empty regions there.

[2] Space is the cause of the universe, but since space pervades everything, it is perceived as confined within the universe.

cause of space, can be encompassed by the body like a jujube in a vessel, much less can a Vedic text which is a valid means of knowledge do so.

As a description of the Puruṣa, it has been said, 'that Puruṣa in whom originate those sixteen parts' (VI. 2). Though that origination of the parts was stated (there) in the Upaniṣad in another connection, still the present text (dealing with creation) is meant to recount the order in which the origination occured as also to show that creation is preceded by intelligence.

स ईक्षांचक्रे। कस्मिन्नहमुत्क्रान्त उत्क्रान्तो भविष्यामि कस्मिन्वा प्रतिष्ठिते प्रतिष्ठास्यामीति ॥३॥

3. He deliberated: 'As a result of whose departure shall I rise up? And as a result of whose continuance shall I remain established?'

Saḥ, He, the Puruṣa endued with sixteen parts, about whom the son of Bharadvāja inquired; *īkṣām cakre*, made this deliberation on, that is to say, penetrated into, the subject of creation, result, order, etc.[1] How he did so is being stated: *Kasmin utkrānte*, which particular agent having risen up, from the body; *bhaviṣyāmi aham*, shall I Myself become; *utkrāntaḥ*, separated? *Vā*, or; *kasmin pratiṣṭhite*, which continuing to be established in the body:

[1] *Creation*—of Prāṇa etc.; *result*—such as their departure from the body; *order*—emergence of faith from Prāṇa and so on; *etc* — the relation of the container and the contained, as subsisting between the world and name etc.

pratiṣṭhāsyāmi aham, shall I remain established? This is the purport.

Objection: Is it not a fact that the Self is not an agent of action, while the Pradhāna (Primal Nature) is? Hence it is the Pradhāna that evolves as Mahat (i.e. the principle of intelligence) and the rest by setting before itself the needs of the Puruṣa (conscious soul). Therefore, in the face of the facts that Pradhāna, existing in a state of balance of its (three) constituents of *sattva* etc., has to be assumed on valid authority to be the creator; that there exist the minutest atoms which act according to Divine Will; that the Self has not the wherewithal to create, It being non-dual; and that the Self cannot be the author of evil to Itself, because a conscious being that acts intelligently cannot do any evil to itself; it is unjustifiable to talk of any agentship of the Puruṣa, preceded by independent deliberation. Accordingly, when, to serve the purposes of the Puruṣa, the insentient Pradhāna evolves in a regular order, as though out of deliberation, the Pradhāna is figuratively spoken of as intelligent in the statement, 'He deliberated' etc., just as one might say, 'He is the king', with regard to an officer who does everything for the king.

Answer: No, since it is as logical to look upon the Self as the doer, as to conceive of It as the enjoyer. Just as from the Sāṁkhya standpoint the Self which is a mere changeless Consciousness can still be the enjoyer, similarly, from the standpoint of the followers of the Vedas, Its creatorship of the world through deliberation can be justified on the authority of the Vedas.

Objection: Any transformation, consisting in a change of (the essence of) the Self into a different category, causes Its impermanence, impurity, and multiplicity; but a mere variation within Its very nature of Consciousness does not do so. Accordingly, if enjoyership is inherent in the Puruṣa Himself, any change within that Consciousness (of enjoyment)[1] is not open to any charge (of mutation of the Self), whereas from your standpoint, who are followers of the Vedas and admit that the Self is the creator, there does occur an essential mutation,[2] and therefore the Self becomes subject to all such faults as impermanence etc.

Answer: No, for it is held by us that though the Self is but one, still, in the state of ignorance, there occur to It apparent distinctions created by the presence or absence of the limiting adjuncts constituted by names and forms of objects. Some sort of a distinction in the Self, created through the limiting adjuncts of name and form that are caused by ignorance, is admitted (as a concession), so that talk about the bondage and freedom of the Self in the scriptures may be possible. In reality, however, what is desired is that one should stand by the unconditioned Entity which is one without a second, which is beyond the reach of all sophists, and which is fearless and auspicious. There can be no agentship, no enjoyership, nor any action, instrument, or result, where everything is reduced to non-duality. The Sāṁkhyas, however, first imagine that agentship, as well as action, instrument, and result, is superimposed on the Self; but as they are outside the pale of the Vedas, they recoil from such a (monistic) position and hold that enjoyership is a real characteristic of the Self. Again, fancying that the Pradhāna is a real substance,

[1] Enjoyment (or suffering) consists in a direct experience of joy (or sorrow). This experience is the very nature of the soul, whereas action belongs to the intellect and the rest.

[2] By becoming the intellect etc. for the purposes of creation.

essentially different from the Self, they fall into the snares woven by the intellect of other (dualistic) sophists and lose their bearing. Similarly are the other sophists led astray by Sāṁkhyas. Thus by postulating theories opposed to each other, like carnivores (fighting for a piece of flesh), they continually drift away from the supreme Reality owing to their proneness to discover such (distorted) interpretations of the conclusions arrived at by valid means of proof as may demolish each other's point of view. Therefore we disclose a few flaws in the theories of the sophists not in the spirit of the sophists, but in order that people desirous of liberation may become devoted to the true import of the Upaniṣads, viz the realization of the non-duality of the Self, by ignoring those other theories. Thus has it been said in this connection: 'Leaving the cause of the origination of all disputes[1] amongst the disputants themselves, and keeping his good sense well protected by their example,[2] the knower of the Vedas reposes happily.'

Moreover, no distinction can be made between the two kinds of modification (in the Self) called enjoyership and agentship. What indeed is that modification characterized as enjoyership which belongs to a class by itself and is different from agentship, depending on which the Puruṣa can be conceived of as merely the enjoyer and not the agent, while the Pradhāna can be thought of as merely an agent and not an enjoyer?

Sāṁkhya: Did we not say that the Puruṣa consists merely of intelligence and that He changes not by being trans-

[1] Apprehension of duality as true.

[2] Having this firm conviction, 'Since the dualistic theories lead only to conflict, non-dualism alone is true.'

formed into some other category, but in the course of experience while still remaining what He is in essence? On the other hand, the Pradhāna changes by being evolved into some other principle, and hence it is possessed of such attributes as multiplicity, impurity, insentience, etc. The Puruṣa is the opposite of it.

Vedāntin: That is a distinction which is not real but merely verbal. If to the Puruṣa, who is (conceived of as) mere intelligence before the emergence of enjoyership, there accrues some special attribute called *experience* at the time of the occurrence of enjoyment, and if after the cessation of the enjoyment, the Puruṣa is freed from that peculiarity and becomes pure intelligence again, (then one may argue that during enjoyment, the enjoying) Pradhāna also evolves as Mahat etc., and then reversing the process (after that experience) it exists in its own nature as Pradhāna. Hence the supposition does not serve to point out any difference. Accordingly, the distinction that is sought to be made between the transformations of the Puruṣa and the Pradhāna is merely a verbal one.

If now it is held that the Puruṣa continues as before to be pure intelligence even during enjoyment, then there is no experience, in the real sense, by the Puruṣa.

Sāṁkhya: The change in the Pure Intelligence during enjoyment is certainly real. Hence, enjoyment is by the Puruṣa.

Vedāntin: That cannot be. Since the Pradhāna too undergoes change during enjoyment, it may as well become the enjoyer.

Sāṁkhya: Change in the pure intelligence alone constitutes enjoyership.

Vedāntin: In that case there is no valid reason why fire

and the rest that are possessed of distinct attributes like heat etc. should not be enjoyers.[1]

Objection: Enjoyership may belong simultaneously to both Pradhāna and Puruṣa.

Vedāntin: No, since in that case the (Sāṁkhya) theory that Pradhāna acts for the benefit of another (viz the Puruṣa) falls through; for among two co-enjoyers there can be no such relationship as overlordship and subordination, just as two lights cannot be so related by way of illuminating each other.

Objection: The enjoyment of the unchanging Puruṣa consists in the production of a reflection of the Puruṣa on the mind-stuff in which the *sattva* quality predominates and which is by nature an enjoyer.

Vedāntin: It cannot be so; for if the Puruṣa is not affected thereby in any way, it is meaningless to posit an enjoyership for Him. If the Puruṣa has no evil in the form of experience, He being ever without attributes, then for removing what (evil) is the (Sāṁkhya) scripture written as a means for emancipation?

Objection: The scripture is written for the sake of removing the evil superimposed through ignorance.

Answer: In that case the hypotheses that in reality the

[1] 'Change in Pure Intelligence alone', may mean two things: (i) change in Intelligence irrespective of any change in another substance; (ii) some uncommon change in the Intelligence alone. The first position is untenable, since the Puruṣa cannot enjoy unless there be corresponding changes in the form of happiness etc. in the Pradhāna. As for the second alternative, there is no special reason why an uncommon change in an uncommon factor, viz Intelligence, should be called enjoyment; for if enjoyment is defined as 'an uncommon change within the thing itself', the definition becomes too wide; and thus fire may also become an enjoyer by a mere uncommon change within its uncommon quality of heat.

Puruṣa is only an enjoyer and not an agent, that the Pradhāna is only a doer and not an enjoyer, and that the Pradhāna is a really existing entity different from the Puruṣa—which (suppositions) are outside the Vedic pale—are useless and unwarranted, and hence need not be taken into consideration by people craving for Liberation.

Objection: Even from the standpoint of non-duality, such activity as the compilation of scriptures is futile.

Answer: No, for no such thing is possible in the state of non-duality. The conflicting thought as to whether the compilation of scriptures is useful or useless can arise only when there are the compilers of the scriptures and others who want to derive some benefit from them; but in the state of non-duality of the Self, apart from the Self there can be no compiler of the scriptures, nor anyone else. And in their absence, this kind of hypothesis itself is altogether unjustifiable. From the very fact of your firm affirmation of the unity of the Self it is admitted by you *pari passu* (from your personal experience) that scriptures serve the valid purpose (of revealing the non-duality of the Self). And the following scriptural text declares with regard to that unity of the Self, to which you subscribe, that when the conviction arises, there is no scope for doubt: 'When to the knower of Brahman everything has become the Self, then what should one see and through what?' (Bṛ.II.iv.14). Similarly in the Vājasaneyaka Upaniṣad it is shown elaborately how in the domain of ignorance which comprises things other than the supreme Reality, it is possible to do such things as the compilation of scriptures: 'Because when there is duality, as it were, (then one sees something)' etc. (*ibid*). Here again, at the very commencement of the scripture (the Upaniṣad of the Atharva Veda, viz

Muṇḍaka. I.i.4), knowledge and ignorance have been separated by calling them higher and lower. Accordingly, the army at the command of sophistic theories cannot enter here into this domain of the non-duality of the Self that is protected by the hands[1] of the king who is none other than the valid proof adduced by Vedānta. It is to be understood that hereby is refuted the fault imputed by others that Brahman lacks the necessary equipment etc. for becoming an agent in the matter of creation etc.; for Brahman can (be imagined to) be associated with differences caused by diverse powers and accessories that emerge from the limiting adjuncts created through name and form which are called up by ignorance. And so also is set aside the other objection raised by others that the Self (of the non-dualists) becomes the originator of Its own misery.[2]

As for the illustration of an officer who does everything for the king and is called by courtesy a king or a master, that has no application here because it runs counter to the (obvious) primary meaning of the Vedic text, 'He deliberated', which is meant to impart valid knowledge; for a secondary meaning of a word is called for only where the primary meaning is inadmissible. But here it does not stand to reason that an insentient entity (viz Pradhāna) should engage in well-regulated activity for the purpose of bondage, liberation, etc. in relation to the Puruṣa, keeping in view the difference between bound and freed souls[3]

[1] The reasoning found in Vedānta.

[2] For God is fancied to be the creator of a world ignorantly superimposed on Him, and He is fancied to ordain good and evil for the souls which have no real separate existence.

[3] That the free souls are to be left apart, and actions are to relate to the bound ones alone.

and taking note of such distinctions as of subject, object, space, time, and causation. On the otherhand, this becomes justifiable from the standpoint already stated that omniscient God is the creator.

By Puruṣa alone, as by a king,[1] is created Prāṇa the director of all. How?

स प्राणमसृजत प्राणाच्छ्रद्धां खं वायुर्ज्योतिरापः पृथिवीन्द्रियं मनः। अन्नमन्नाद्वीर्यं तपो मन्त्राः कर्म लोका लोकेषु च नाम च ॥४॥

4. He created Prāṇa; from Prāṇa (He created) faith, space, air, fire, water, earth, organs, mind, food; from food (He created) vigour, self-control, *mantras*, rites, worlds, and name in the worlds.

Having deliberated in the way stated before, *saḥ*, He, the Puruṣa; *asṛjata*, created; *prāṇam*, Prāṇa,[2] (the sum total of all Prāṇas,) called Hiraṇyagarbha,[3] that is the repository of the organs of all beings, and is the inner soul of all.[4] From this Prāṇa, He created *śraddhām*, faith, that is the source of stimulus for all beings for good action.

[1] This is according to the reading '*Īśvareṇa iva*'. An alternative reading is, '*Īśvareṇa eva*, by God Himself (who is Puruṣa).'

[2] Energy, both mental (i.e. intellectual) and physical.

[3] That is to say, the limiting adjunct through which the Self appears to be individualized and comes to be known as Hiraṇyagarbha A.G.

[4] As the sum total of all the subtle bodies, this limiting adjunct, called Hiraṇyagarbha, resides inside the gross bodies and is thought of as one's self. Hence it is *antar*, inside, and *ātman*, self.

From that He created the great elements that support by becoming the material constituents of the (physical body that is the) vehicle of enjoyment of the fruits of actions. (He created) *kham*, space, possessed of the quality of sound; *vāyuḥ*, air, possessed of two attributes, its own attribute of touch and the attribute (sound) of its source (space); similarly *jyotiḥ*, fire, possessed of three qualities—its own quality of colour and the qualities of sound and touch belonging to the earlier two; similarly *āpaḥ*, water, possessed of four attributes—its own individual quality of taste and the infusion of the three earlier qualities (sound, touch, colour); similarly *pṛthivī*, earth, endowed with five qualities by virtue of its possession of smell, and the permeation of the four earlier qualities (sound, touch, colour, taste). So also (He created) *indriyam*, the organs—constituted by those elements themselves—, which are of two kinds and are ten in number for the purposes of perception and action; and (He created) *manaḥ*, the mind, the lord of those organs, which resides inside and is characterized by doubt and thought. Having thus created the body and the organs of the creatures, He created for their sustenance *annam*, food, constituted by paddy, barley, etc. *Annāt*, from that food, when eaten; (He created) *vīryam*, ability, vigour that is at the root of engaging in all works. After that (He created) *tapaḥ*, self control, for the sake of the purification of those strong creatures who get involved in the intermixture of castes (through sin). Then (He created) *mantrāḥ*, mantras, comprising the *Ṛk*, *Yajur*, *Sāma*, and *Atharva* texts, which are the means of (religious) activities for those who have purified their internal and external organs with the help of self-control; then *karma*, rites, such as Agnihotra; then *lokāḥ*, the worlds, the results of rites. And in these worlds He created *nāma*, names, for instance Devadatta or Yajñadatta, of the created beings. Thus, in conformity with[1] the seeds constituted by such defects of the creatures as ignorance, these parts were created—like two moons, mosquitoes, bees, etc. created by the blurred vision of a man suffering from the disease called Timira, or like all sorts of things created by a dreamer—, and these again merge into that very Puruṣa by giving up such distinctions of name, form, etc.

How?

स यथेमा नद्यः स्यन्दमानाः समुद्रायणाः समुद्रं प्राप्यास्तं गच्छन्ति भिद्येते तासां नामरूपे समुद्र इत्येवं प्रोच्यते। एवमेवास्य परिद्रष्टुरिमाः षोडश कलाः पुरुषायणाः पुरुषं प्राप्यास्तं गच्छन्ति भिद्येते चासां नामरूपे पुरुष इत्येवं प्रोच्यते स एषोऽकलोऽमृतो भवति तदेष श्लोकः ॥५॥

5. The illustration is this: Just as these flowing rivers that have the sea as their goal, get absorbed after reaching the sea, and their names and forms are destroyed, and they are called merely the sea, so also these sixteen parts (i.e. the constituents) of the all-seeing Puruṣa, that have the Puruṣa as their goal, disappear on reaching the Puruṣa, when their names and forms are destroyed and they are simply called as Puruṣa. Such a man of realization becomes free from the parts and is immortal. On this point there occurs this verse:

Saḥ, the illustration is this: In the world, *yathā*, as;

[1] Taking them as His aid.

imāḥ, these; *syandamānāḥ nadyaḥ*, flowing rivers; *samudrāyaṇāḥ*, that have the sea as their goal, the place where they get absorbed; *samudraṁ prāpya*, after reaching the sea; *gacchanti astam*, court disappearance, lose their names and forms;—and *tāsām nāma-rupe*, the names of those (rivers), for instance, Gangā, Yamunā, etc., that have become absorbed; *bhidyete*, get eliminated; and, as a result of that merger, their substance that is water, *samudraḥ iti evam procyate*, is called merely by the word sea;—*evam*, similarly, as is this illustration, so; *asya*, of that Puruṣa, who is possessed of the attributes mentioned before, and who is being considered here; *paridraṣṭuḥ*, of Him who is the seer on all sides, who is the agent of a vision that is identical with His real nature, just as the sun is everywhere the agent of the light that is identical with itself; *imāḥ ṣoḍaśa-kalāḥ*, these sixteen parts—the parts, counting from Prāṇa, that have been mentioned; *puruṣāyaṇāḥ*, which have the Puruṣa as their goal, the place where they get identified, as the sea is with relation to the rivers; *prāpya puruṣam*, on reaching the Puruṣa, on getting identified with the Puruṣa; *astam gacchanti*, disappear, in that very manner; *ca*, and; *āsām*, of them, of the parts; the respective *nāma-rūpe*, names such as Prāṇa, as well as forms; *bhidyete*, get destroyed. When names and forms are eliminated, the entity that remains undestroyed, *procyate*, is called, by the knowers of Brahman; *puruṣaḥ iti evam*, as Puruṣa. *Saḥ*, he, who has become thus enlightened after being shown by his teacher the process of the absorption of the parts; *bhavati*, becomes; *akalaḥ*, free from the parts, when the parts, viz Prāṇa and the rest that are the creation of ignorance, desire, and action, are absorbed through knowledge; (and he becomes *amṛtaḥ*, immortal). Death is a creation of the parts originating from nescience. When those parts are gone, one becomes immortal just because of one's partlessness. *Tat*, with regard to this matter; *bhavati*, there occurs; *eṣaḥ ślokaḥ*, this verse:

अरा इव रथनाभौ कला यस्मिन्प्रतिष्ठिताः ।
तं वेद्यं पुरुषं वेद यथा मा वो मृत्युः परिव्यथा इति ॥६॥

6. You should know that Puruṣa who is worthy to be known and in whom are transfixed the parts like spokes in the nave of a chariot wheel, so that death may not afflict you anywhere.

Iva, as; *arāḥ*, spokes, which are, as it were, the dependants of a chariot wheel; *pratiṣṭhitāḥ*, are transfixed; *rathanābhau*, in the nave of a chariot wheel; that is to say, as they are dependent on the hub, so; *veda*, one should know; *tam vedyam puruṣam*, that knowable Puruṣa, who is the self of the parts (limbs) and who is called Puruṣa because of all-pervasiveness or existence in the city (i.e. *pur* of the body); *yasmin*, in whom, in which Puruṣa; *pratiṣṭhitāḥ*, are transfixed; the *kalāḥ*, parts (limbs), during the states of origin, continuance, and dissolution. (You know Him) *yathā*, so that; O disciples, *mṛtyuḥ*, death; *mā vaḥ parivyathāḥ*, may not afflict you on any side. If the Puruṣa remains unknown, you will continue to be miserable under pain inflicted by death. Hence, may that not fall to your lot. This is the idea.

तान् होवाचैतावदेवाहमेतत् परं ब्रह्म वेद। नातः परमस्तीति ॥७॥

7. To them he said, 'I know this supreme Brahman thus far only. Beyond this there is nothing.'

Having thus instructed them (i.e. the disciples), Pippalāda *uvāca ha*, said; *tān*, to them, to those disciples; '*Veda*, I know; *etāvat eva*, thus far only; *etat*, this; *param brahma*, supreme Brahman, that is worthy to be known. *Ataḥ param*, beyond this; *na asti*, there is not—anything higher to be known.' Thus did he say this in order to remove from the disciples any doubt that there might still remain something unknown; and also in order to generate in them the conviction that they had attained the final goal.

It is being stated what those disciples did when they found no recompense for their knowledge after being taught by the teacher and getting their purposes fulfilled:

ते तमर्चयन्तस्त्वं हि नः पिता योऽस्माकमविद्यायाः परं पारं
तारयसीति। नमः परमऋषिभ्यो नमः परमऋषिभ्यः ॥८॥

इति प्रश्नोपनिषदि षष्ठः प्रश्नः ॥

8. While worshipping him they said, 'You indeed are our father who have ferried us across nescience to the other shore. Salutation to the great seers. Salutation to the great seers.'

It is being stated what; *te*, they said; *arcayantaḥ*, while worshipping his feet by offering handfuls of flowers and saluting him with their heads: '*Tvam hi*, you indeed are; *naḥ*, our; *pitā*, father, since you have generated through knowledge a (fresh) birth in Brahman that is eternal, ageless, deathless, and fearless. Since it is you who, with the help of the raft of knowledge, have ferried us *avidyāyāḥ param pāram*, across ignorance or false knowledge—as though across an ocean itself, infested with birth, old age, death, disease, sorrow, etc., which are like sea animals—, to the other shore of the boundless ocean of nescience, called emancipation, consisting in absolute cessation of rebirth; therefore your fatherhood towards us is more justifiable than that of the others (i.e. our real fathers). The other father, who begets the body alone, is yet the most worshipful in the world, what to speak of one who guarantees absolute fearlessness? This is the purport. *Namaḥ*, salutation; *paramarṣibhyaḥ*, to the great seers, the originators of the line of traditional transmission of the knowledge of Brahman. The repetition of *namaḥ paramarṣibhyaḥ* is for showing respect.

ॐ भद्रं कर्णेभिः श्रृणुयाम देवा
भद्रं पश्येमाक्षभिर्यजत्राः ।
स्थिरैरङ्गैस्तुष्टुवाꣳसस्तनूभि-
र्व्यशेम देवहितं यदायुः ॥

ॐ शान्तिः शान्तिः शान्तिः ॥

INDEX TO THE SECTIONS